The Joy of Christian Fathering

The Joy of
Christian Fathering

Five First-Person Accounts

Compiled and Edited by
DONALD N. BASTIAN

Light and Life Press
Winona Lake, Indiana

ISBN: 0-919532-36-5

© 1980 G.R. Welch Company, Ltd.

Published by Free Methodist Publishing House
Light and Life Press
Winona Lake, Indiana
46590

Published in Canada by G.R. Welch Company, Ltd.
Burlington, Ontario
L7L 5K7

Printed in Canada

to
Kathleen
and to
Edna
Deloris
Sherry
and
Dorothy

Five women who helped make Christian
fathering a possibility and a joy.

Contents

Acknowledgments   viii

A Father Remembered   ix

The Joy of Christian Fathering   1

John Benson   9

  W. Dale Cryderman   27

  Paul N. Ellis   45

  Hugh A. White   61

  Donald N. Bastian   77

Epilogue   99

viii

Acknowledgments

Paul, Dale, John and Hugh are four friends who are both interesting to know and easy to admire. Busy though they are, they responded readily when I asked them to tell their stories in this book.

Donald Gregory, my editor son who himself will be a father before this volume is published, went over its pages with me and offered helpful suggestions.

Kathleen, Sherry, Dorothy, Deloris and Edna, five women who helped the five men in this book to look good in front of their children, are deserving of acknowledgments beyond any we five can give. They tend to be quiet people, but they have a moral strength you couldn't break with a jackhammer.

Two very special people who themselves are the parents of children surging toward adulthood deserve thanks. Although they wish to remain unnamed, they generously provided funds to speed the book along.

I must acknowledge as a class scores of fathers I have learned about through this project. They've stolen no headlines and appeared on no television talk shows but they are men who rank high with their children. There ought to be a tomb of the Unknown Christian Father!

My secretary, Barbara Sackett, treated drafts of these chapters, plus a heavy correspondence, with a remarkable combination of technical skill and fortitude.

Above all others, I humbly acknowledge the One who is "the father from whom every family in heaven and on earth is named" and whom the apostle Paul identifies as "the God and Father of our Lord Jesus Christ."

A Father Remembered

My father emigrated from the coalfields of Lancashire, England, to the coalfields of southeastern Saskatchewan shortly after the turn of the century.

He was a small man — five-feet-four-inches tall, weighing scarcely more than one hundred pounds.

Behind him, in the Lancashire village of Stubsha Cross, he left the prospect of a life of certain poverty. The prairies of western Canada promised little more, though he came to make his fortune.

At eighteen he was energetic and determined, committed to the work ethic, and confident that with diligence and toil he could more than make his way in the New World.

He once described to me the extent of his formal education. At five years of age, he had been sent to school. A few weeks later he came down with scarlet fever, was taken out of school and never sent back.

At thirteen he had gone into the labyrinthine Lancashire mines to be his father's helper. From then on during the winter he saw daylight only on Sundays! In old age his nightmares continued to have their setting in the horrors of those mines.

Even before that, at nine years of age, his father sent him and an older sister during the summer to staff a fish and chip cart pulled by a worn-out nag. I remember his account of the peril both occasionally were in from encounters with drunken miners.

Yet he taught himself to read, write and do basic arithmetic. I remember when I was growing up how he pored over the editorial page of the Regina Leader. I saw him at the kitchen table working with columns of figures. By the time of his retirement at sixty-three he had advanced from the mines to a market garden, to the establishment of a small bakery in Estevan, and finally to the ownership and management of a furniture exchange.

He lived to the ripe old age of eighty-three, a Canadian by choice but an Englishman to the end. Sixty-five years in Canada scarcely blunted the delightful Lancashire dialect spoken in a lilting tenor voice. In the closing years of his life he could still speak jauntily in one sentence about the 'air on your 'ead, and in the next about the "hair" in the "hatmosphere."

He passed easily from this life while sweeping a bit of snow from his doorstep. The word came to me halfway across the continent only thirty-six days after I had stood at his side for my mother's funeral.

During the dozen years since that news came, I have reviewed the memories of my childhood — allowing for unavoidable distortions and erasures. I know the past was never quite the way it now seems. Nevertheless, I have identified to my own satisfaction the most important contributions my father made to my life.

He made my human existence possible. That alone is reason enough for gratitude. But going beyond the physical fact of paternity, his contributions fall into the category of *fatherhood* — what a man attempts to do in positive ways for a child whose existence he has made possible.

He dandled me on his foot when I was little more than an infant. Later, my sister, three-and-a-half years younger, had the same experience while I stood enviously by. That's how I know. I assume all five of us children enjoyed "horseyback" — an early and primitive version of today's Jolly Jumper but with the added benefit of intimate parent-child contact.

When I was a schoolboy, perhaps nine, my father got on his knees midway between the old coal heater and davenport in our modest living room and taught me to box. He had learned the skill in mining camps. There were gales of laughter from the sidelines as I bobbed and weaved and ducked to no avail. His hands were lightning fast.

I remember too the Model A Ford truck he used for deliveries. After hours, he perched my sister and me on apple boxes in the bed hard against the cab and drove us to the prairie at the edge of town. We played catch. As dusk approached there we were, three little people against the backdrop of a big western sky, the wind singing incessantly in the long grass.

My father was unusually athletic, an aptitude which none of his five children can boast. He enjoyed himself immensely at such community events as church picnics, challenging the younger people in all kinds of sports. I myself remember when, past fifty, he discovered softball and was soon pitcher for his team.

Once when he was about fifty-two and I ten (according to my best calculations) we were walking together along Thirteenth Street in my home town of Estevan going north. With childish enthusiasm I said, "Let's race." He bolted forward and together we ran pell-mell along the sidewalk toward the railroad station.

There were no expensive gifts in my early years, no fantastic vacations, no clothing allowances, no steak barbecues. Heavy home-baked brown bread dipped in fried tomatoes was a fare I remember with unusual vividness. Depression time was survival time. Nor was life without its childhood nightmares. Childhood is always laced with anxieties and hurts and growing up is not an easy assignment.

Yet, in simple things — foot races, games of catch, even his letting me sit on his lap to steer the car along a gravel road — Dad made big investments in my future. Experiences like these must have nudged me toward manhood. They certainly gave me the sense that it is good to be a man. Talk about confused sexual identity we hear so much these days awakens in me a deep sense of gratitude for the male-orientation that came through from my father. I'm certain, moreover, that these simple father-child exchanges had a strong bearing on my own later joy at being a father.

Dad was not a Christian all the years of my youth. At least not by evangelical standards. Only when he was past sixty did he make the move that startled and pleased us all. But as far back as I can remember, twice on Sunday he went with the family to church. I continued to attend church through the high dropout years of the early teens, and at sixteen years of age was converted. Although my mother's Christian influence was primary in this, my father's example was a factor too.

Dad never raised a hand to discipline us. That fell the lot of my petite but forceful mother. She filled the part of two parents with her diligent combination of a leather strap that hung behind the kitchen door and certain verses of Scripture that suffered from overuse.

Dad threatened occasionally to give us children a "backhander," a word he must have brought with him from Lancashire, and when he became exasperated, he made threatening gestures of taking off his belt. But after two or three false starts, we soon learned these threats would not materialize. Looking back through the mist of the years, I think a strong male hand in the home would have been a valuable asset. It would have made for greater order.

However, all homes are deficient in one way or another, and from the perspective of half a century, I cherish my father's positive contributions to my life more than I regret the lack of male discipline. If I had to choose between the two I'd take what I got, although the ideal would include a blend of both. He cared in the ways he was skilled in caring. He wanted what was right for us and he used the fathering resources he had. If he had known more, I'm sure he would have done more.

In one sense my father has been gone a dozen years. In another sense, he is still inside me. This book must have been conceived, at least in part, as a result of his influence on my life. I honor him for the good he did and the greater good he intended.

The Joy of Christian Fathering

I first shared my idea of a book on Christian fathering with a group of young men at a seminar for graduate students in religion. We were standing in a circle and talking informally in the large red-carpeted lounge of International Friendship House, Winona Lake, Indiana. It was coffee break time. Each of us ceremoniously held the usual white styrofoam cup in hand as relaxed conversation drifted from one interest to another.

I was thinking, I told them, of having four "battle-scarred" fathers join me in writing about our fathering experiences. Each of us would contribute one chapter, recalling delights and disappointments we had known in helping to raise our offspring. We would try not to be preachy although I wouldn't want to stop our values and opinions from shining through. Our chapters would be essentially first-person accounts.

I detected instant interest in the circle. Most of the men, though young, were married, and some had children.

"Hey," one man said with enthusiasm, "you're talking about having five men share some contemporary wisdom." He went on, "You know, we're losing our wisdom. Right now I'm writing down all sorts of wise things my father said to me so I can be sure to pass them on to my four-year-old son as he gets old enough to handle them." This man is a seminary professor.

Stimulated by the response, I shared my idea with other men in places as far separated as Alberta, California and Brazil.

"I want to read that book," several responded in identical words, though continents apart.

"Hurry up," one young husband said as he stood beside his wife in an Alberta church yard, "our first child will be here in two months." Grinning, he laid his hand gently on his wife's protuberant tummy.

A decade earlier young husbands would not have been so quick to show interest. At the close of the turbulent 1960s things were quite different. I was a college pastor at that time. I remember that the youth generation seemed more interested in talking than listening. There were exceptions, but generally they acted confident of themselves and distrustful of their elders.

I don't mean to imply that everything that came out of the '60s was bad. For one thing, the feminist movement, ascending during that decade, helped to break up the rigid stereotypes about what fathers and mothers do in the family. This has released many men to participate more in the nurturing aspects of raising children. They no longer feel they have to be strong and silent, out of the feeling range of little ones.

But in these intervening years we all seem to have become more *aware* of the bad things happening to families in the western world. Wherever I go I now find young parents anxious and uneasy. Perhaps we are seeing the increasing brittleness of family bonds and in the face of this our self-sufficiency is wearing thin. In our questions about family matters now, humility is more evident. And there seems to be a rising willingness to discuss Christian fathering.

As I write this my own son Donald and my son-in-law Douglas are about to become fathers. They are approaching the task with confidence and joy but I have detected in both of them a "seeking" for guidance. Each is unabashedly prayerful about the advent of a first child, and each goes with his wife to the prenatal classes — eager to learn from whomever can instruct him.

The desire for a recovery of wisdom seems to be spreading, especially in the church, and it should. Realism demands it. A little reflection will bring to mind that there are all kinds of fathers just as there are all kinds of drivers. A devoted Christian can be a poor driver, can he not? He can also, then, be an ineffectual father. A Christian father has to be more than a father who is a Christian. At least, an *effective* Christian father does. That calls for wisdom.

I assume you agree with me that Christian fathering requires a solid commitment to Jesus Christ, since such a commitment is basic to being a Christian at all. But, effective Christian fathering also requires skills that are learned, and devotion to the task. As good drivers must learn to drive, good fathers must learn to father. In either endeavor, those who are content merely to follow their intuitions or blind conditioning may end up in the ditch.

It seemed to me, therefore, that given the new climate of humility with regard to the Christian family, five seasoned Christian fathers might get a ready hearing. They could talk about their experiences as fathers in such a way that young husbands could "look over their shoulders," evaluate what they were "seeing" and take away any insights that made sense to them.

In thinking about this book, that's all I planned from the start. No lectures. No organized lessons in psychology. No preaching or pomposity. Not even gems of wisdom, though you might find some things here that can be reduced to aphorisms for posterity. All I promise you are incidents and observations out of the crucible of five lively families, delivered to us by five veteran fathers.

So I picked four fathers, in addition to myself, but not until I had set the following criteria: they must all be fathers of children who are now grown, say, at least to the age of twenty-five. They must be fathers whose children are all committed to Jesus Christ and who are serving Him in the fellowship of His church here on earth. Their children must all be functioning well in the life of society.

Together, the five of us have fathered seventeen children. Among them are teachers, doctors, executives, writers, preachers, builders, professors and homemakers.

Among the seventeen children is one who does not meet the criteria. You will learn about him in due course. The outcome of his life entails great disappointment on the part of his parents but they have come to terms with their grief. They've also learned something from the experience and in one respect the child has been their teacher.

So, meet the first father, John C. Benson, father of four.

John made moon rockets and tree houses with his growing sons and cheered them on as they built and raced soapbox cars. A printer by trade, he knows his field from ems to offset presses, and he uses a camera with the skill of a professional. He has a way with words too, as I think you'll see.

Meet W. Dale Cryderman. He was a photographer with the Detroit Times when God tapped him on the shoulder, turned him around spiritually and directed him toward the ministry. He has never lost his fascination with newspapers, and the strong human interest you'll sense in his chapter may be a permanent residue of his first career with the media.

Meet Paul N. Ellis. Mathematics, psychology and theology are only some of the subjects he has put under the examination of his penetrating mind. Crowned by a handsome head of snow white hair, he lives intensely and reads widely and from this regimen has formed clear convictions about life.

Meet Hugh A. White, a tall and energetic certified public accountant whose experience in the financial world has been too wide-ranging to chart here. His skill in investments is broadly recognized. But it will be seen here that Hugh's most important investments have been made in his family and his church.

And meet me, the father of four and a Canadian whose concern to strengthen family life has been deepened by twenty-one years as a pastor in the United States and Canada. The oldest of my children, my petite daughter Carolyn, has a practical turn of mind and has been immensely helpful in recalling with me our experiences as a growing family.

The five of us fathers range in age from fifty-three to seventy-seven. Hugh A. White holds the position of seniority among us and may be the most energetic as well. I am the youngest. At my request we have written without comparing notes. As the manuscripts came in, only I knew what all the fathers were saying. If you find common emphases in our stories, they must be attributed to some common heritage.

You'll see we're different from one another and our interests vary widely. But we have important things in common. For example, we're all committed men — unabashedly so. This, in spite of the fact that commitment at the present is not widely regarded as a good thing because it is said to hamper freedom. All five of us are committed to God as he has made himself known in Jesus Christ, and to all five, Jesus is not only a historical person but a personal presence as well.

We are also committed to our wives, children, church and jobs. Two of us are even avid golfers although commitment may be too strong a word for this interest. There are no fanatics among us, not even golf fanatics.

Looking back now on the years when our families made the greatest demands upon us, we realize that busy though we were, God gave us enough time to do everything in life that was important. It took a bit of planning and sorting. The trivial was always there bidding to take over. Sometimes when family life began to get out of focus for us, priorities had to be reordered, putting the trivial in its place. In all this, we found commitment a liberating ally, not a foe!

We also have in common that we did not perform perfectly as fathers. Fortunately a man does not have to perform perfectly to be an effective Christian father, and our children — a forgiving lot — have not expected it. All twenty-seven of us, five fathers, five mothers and seventeen children, know that a Christian home is a place where forgiveness is often received and given.

What we five have most in common is the experience of joy. We were harried at times when the children were growing up. More than that; before the task was done we were baffled, perplexed, surprised, dumbfounded, astonished, flabbergasted, hurt, dazzled, silenced, outwitted, disconcerted and rattled. The memories of these moments have all but washed out of our consciousness. It would take truth serum or deep hypnosis to bring them up. But the residue of joy which was there all the time, remains.

There were also times when happiness — felt with a certain male restraint — was nearly boundless. For example when watching a small child show his first generosity with a cookie or listening to an offspring play a simple version of the William Tell Overture at a piano recital. The happiness of those moments quickly faded but the joy remained. Across the whole range of feelings that fathering produced, we were supported by the tough grace called joy.

A handwritten saying that's been around our house for several years puts the matter simply. One of our sons captured it in a college chapel service, wrote it on an index card and taped it to the filing cabinet beside his desk. Tenaciously it hung there by one strand of Scotch tape, surviving even an eight hundred mile truck ride from southern Illinois to Toronto. It's still around our house. It says, "When you do that which is your responsibility, joy will overtake you on the path."

We five have tried to carry out our responsibility. God's grace has enabled us to do so and for every success we give him credit. But we know that, undergirded by his grace, we have done the marching, and in marching along this path of Christian fathering, joy has often overtaken us. This is a book that reflects the joy.

Start a boy on the right road, and even in old age he will not leave it.

Proverbs 22:6 NEB

SOME OF THE STRATEGIES and tactics of life were built into their boys via the game of chess. Sherry and John Benson won a few games — until the young men got the hang of it! Left to right, Sherry, Dan, Paul, Jay, John, and Dale.

John C. Benson

John C. Benson *knows and loves the printing business. His interest in linotypes and T-squares was first whetted in a print shop during college days in Iowa. Now in his retirement, he keeps his hand in printing by working at World Missionary Press in New Paris, a community north of Winona Lake, Indiana, where he and his wife Sherry live.*

But he is a man of many gifts, and in 1959 his church sent him to India where he designed and installed a modern water system for Umri Mission Hospital. He regards this as his highest and most satisfying achievement to date.

John and Sherry's oldest son Dale, and his wife Barb, live in Indianapolis, Indiana, where as a medical doctor he directs several neighborhood health centers along with a drug abuse treatment center in the inner city.

Their second son Jay is assistant to the president of World Missionary Press, an organization that produces literature for overseas mission fields and which has in process at all times literature in forty-five new languages. Jay and his wife Vicky earlier spent time as literature missionaries in Indonesia.

Their third son Paul, and his wife Barbara, also reside in Indianapolis where he is employed as a construction supervisor. Earlier, he was a professor of music at Central College, McPherson, Kansas.

Dan, their youngest son, author of The Total Man, *lives with his wife Kathy in Denver, Colorado, where he is book editor for Accent Publications.* The Total Man *has been a best-seller.*

John's skill in printing is well known to his friends. Those who know his boys respect him also for the good imprint he has left on them.

If there is one statement I could make about raising a family that would sum it all up, it would go something like this: raising a family can be noisy, exciting, expensive, demanding and rewarding — but never dull. I never knew what to expect next. I don't know about girls, but boys are definitely boisterous!

Before our first child arrived, I doubt I would have been brash enough to write to anyone about raising children. And even now, in no way do I pose as any kind of an expert. The boys aborning selected appropriate genes, an adequate environment, godly grandparents, and parents who were ignorant but willing to learn. For all of us, it was an invigorating experience in togetherness.

The catapult that launched our parenting career was, of course, the birth of Dale. The cloak of fatherhood had been dropped on my shoulders, and in spite of the love and joy I felt over his arrival, my shoulders were shaking. Dale was here. What do we do with him? Chickens and animals I had raised. But little people, no.

It didn't take long to find out the baby knew all about us: how to tell us when he was happy, hungry, uncomfortable and sleepy; how to awaken us in the night and negate our irritation by grasping a finger with a strong, miniature hand; and how to rearrange family schedules and priorities so he could stay at the top.

Several sessions of Dale's vocal practice from two until three in the morning at our home in Peoria, Illinois, gave rise to second thoughts about the business of being a father; but fortunately for all of us, we were well past the place of making that decision.

In Peoria, his younger brother Jay joined us and then, when we were living in Texas, along came Paul. The final part in the "choir" was filled by Dan, who was born in Prairie City, Iowa. When he was three, we moved to Winona Lake, Indiana, where we raised our family.

One of my youngsters helped me strengthen faith in myself. One day I looked into his wide, blue, confident eyes and something in me said: "Son, you're looking to me for love and protection, for food to eat, for clothes to wear, for shoes to take you to school, for advice and encouragement as you enter this exciting game of life . . . I won't let you down . . . I'll study and work and plan and pray to provide everything your childlike trust expects of me." I remember this because it was printed in the *Prairie City News,* a weekly newspaper we owned and published for four years.

I recall one of our little cyclones, about eighteen months old, "helping" me in the workshop while I tried to build a shelf. My accomplishment in one hour: sawed a board too short and nailed it on crooked. Son's accomplishment: mixed six sizes of nails together, dumped my screw assortment on the floor, spilled liquid glue, puddled on my hammer handle, and climbed the attic steps several times to throw rocks at me from a stone collection. I began to understand why the house and furniture and Sherry were beginning to show signs of wear.

One balmy spring day we took a two-year-old out into the yard. I wondered what thoughts went through his little mind as he pulled and patted the grass . . . as he started chasing a fat robin that kept a few jumps ahead . . . when he picked up a handful of sand and let the cool grains run out through his fingers . . . while taking his first ride on the swing . . . and when he followed an airplane across the sky with his eyes and comments. Wouldn't it be great if a child could have our vocabulary for a little while and describe all these original sensations?

I stood in awe at the frequent displays of the boys' imaginations. Wide-eyed and serious, they explained complicated plans or did something that seemed "way out." Usually the ideas were a little weird from an adult standpoint, but they were no doubt very plausible to their authors. I had heard that parents should guide, but not curb, the imagination of their children but I wondered just what and how much direction should be supplied. Was it not out of fantastic imaginations that came the steam engine, the airplane and wonder drugs? I decided a child's healthy imagination has got to be just as important as his healthy body.

Of course, when a six-year-old boy winds up a small car and places it on the head of his little brother, the ensuing snarl makes a parent wonder if he really wants to let imaginations run *that* rampant!

When all four boys were romping around the house and yard, one of Sherry's and my most obvious goals was that of day-to-day survival — how to keep meals and clean clothing ready when needed and our sanity intact.

But there were other goals, not sharply defined at the time, but which have become apparent in retrospect:

• *To transfer our hard-come-by set of values to the boys by a maximum of practice and a minimum of preaching.*
It would have scared us silly at the time had Sherry and I realized that children start picking up ideas and actions from their parents when they are only a few weeks old. Long before they start kindergarten their life direction and many of their habits and attitudes are pretty firmly fixed. I don't remember how my wife and I talked or behaved way back then, but if the above is true, we can pretty well see ourselves by taking an objective look (is it possible?) at our offspring. If they're on the right track, God be praised!

Paul, at age three, was listening to a serious exhortation I was giving on the evils of playing in the mud. It went something like this: "We mustn't play in the mud Paul. We get our hands dirty and our faces all muddy. It gets on our feet and gets tracked into the house, and we get our clothes all dirty." Whereupon little quick-on-the-trigger came back with: "Daddy, you've got a dirty shirt!"

Paul comments now that it is important that parents be convinced that what they are doing is important and valuable — and pass on the delight to the children — the delight of accomplishment.

• *To expose them to our various skills and interests to see if anything would develop on the 400-plus ASA film of their eager minds.*
Sherry and I have always loved to read. It gives us something extra to think and talk about. From a decorator's point of view, our house has been a disaster area for years. There were good books and magazines within arm's reach of every chair and bed — many of them open or with "in use" markers. It was surprising how much reading we did in snatches — that's about all the time that's left when the house is full of vivacious little people. The boys picked up

the habit, and today all of them are medium-to-avid readers. Who is to know which books have influenced us? and them? and in which directions?

Of course I invited them into my workshop; any basic skills they might develop would come in handy later. But the skill that sprouted first was in carrying my tools out into the yard and losing them. That problem was solved by my hanging them (the tools, that is) higher and higher so they wouldn't be so free to travel. The boys built rudimentary airplanes and boats; then cars, shelves, bird houses. Eventually each son built two or more Soap Box Derby racing cars, and today Paul is building houses.

- *To keep our Christianity an integral part of our daily lives, so that it would be completely natural for all of us to have love for and confidence in God. To make the practice of prayer a personal habit.*

One of our sons, who now says that going to church was never a problem for him, made this comment when he was six: "I liked going to my Uncle Stanley's church because it lasted shorter."

Each of our children was committed to God before he was born, and prayed for and with daily after his arrival. It is a strange phenomenon, this business of being a parent; it starts but it never stops. Like Ol' Man River, it just keeps rollin' along. Our prayers for the boys (and now for their wives and families) have never stopped. We love and care and pray as much as ever. Maybe more.

Sherry and I wondered how we could be positive without being pushy in training our family in the area of personal religion. Gradually we found some things that helped:

— We looked for the goodness in every child. Sometimes this took a bit of searching, but we kept looking. There were nuggets of character showing through the mischievous chinks. We tried to accentuate the positive, and to think of ways to demonstrate God's love through things we said and did. A smile, an arm across the shoulders, a note in the lunch box. There were all kinds of ways. The child who was most distressing probably needed a vote of confidence most.

— We recognized each child as a person of worth, whom we tried to treat at least as courteously as someone outside our home. We tried never to belittle a child, particularly when he was with other children. Instead, we built him up at every opportunity.

— Child-level crises come fast and furious, often at unexpected times. We tried to understand why certain situations were so traumatic, and to have some kind of satisfactory plan, answer, or Band Aids ready.

— We bent with the blows. When five family members all had to have supper at different times, we tried not to make a federal crime out of it. Their varied interests made our home at times look like Grand Central Station, but it didn't necessarily shamble our nerves.

All of us believed in God, but took Him pretty much for granted, until a flash fire ejected us into the street on a stormy April night. Dale and Jay were rescued unconscious and spent a week in a hospital. The rest of us got out safely, but the trauma of having our new home betray us — as well as the loss of many irreplaceable personal items — drew us closer to each other and to God, and away from the "deceitfulness" of earthly possessions.

Dale has said to me: "I was impressed with how much you loved and cared for me. It strengthened our family."

Jay has written:

Perhaps more than at any other time during my youth I sensed my Dad's love for me when near tragedy struck our family. My older brother Dale and I were trapped in our basement bedroom by fire in the middle of the night, caused by lightning setting a blaze in the furnace room outside our door. We jumped out of bed and began yelling against the rain and thunderstorm raging outside, "Dad, help us! Dad, help us!"

We were answered only by the sound of pounding rain, as choking smoke filled our lungs. Even as we became unconscious and fell to the floor, Dad was fighting for our lives. He had run to the back of the house, smashed the window of the furnace room, and put the fire out with a garden hose. Firemen arrived and were able to rescue us only by using Scott Air-Paks which had been received and tested just three days previously. When I regained consciousness a little later in a neighbor's house, Dad was sitting on the bed beside me waiting, hoping, praying — and when I saw him and his loving smile, my heart was touched deeply.

Both Dale and Jay in personal testimonies have told how the fire was a turning point for the better in their spiritual lives.

But through it all my spirits were completely demoralized. Working day after day to get the house in shape to live in again, I felt very much alone, as if even God didn't care. I didn't share these feelings with Sherry or the boys because I didn't want to undermine their courage.

When the boys came home from hospital, as a family we gradually and cautiously reestablished communications with God through prayer and praise. At first we were fearful that He had allowed this to happen to us to teach us something, and Sherry and I at least were hesitant because we thought we might have completely missed whatever God wanted us to learn. But things came into focus as the weeks went by. By the time we moved back into the house, we were quite sure the main lesson God wanted to teach us right then was that the most helpful factor in raising a family is daily communication with God about everything. He heard and helped. That lesson we learned, but good.

Dale and Jay also had the beginnings of their Soap Box Derby cars wiped out by the fire. They even made that a matter of prayer as they started over. Come July, Jay won the B event (for younger boys) and Dale the A. Then Dale took the runoff and went on to compete in the international event in Akron, Ohio, in August.

- *To invest ourselves totally in the lives of those four receptive little human beings God had loaned to us for a few years. To guide. To encourage. To maintain a keen interest in everything that each accomplished.*

Sherry developed a unique way of letting me invest myself in my boys. On Fathers' Day she went away and left me at home with the brood. Very educational, to say the least. I also found out that if I were to keep my "public relations" with the boys by giving them cookies, I for sure must have the same number of cookies as boys, otherwise the P.R. went noisily out the window.

In one of my attempts to maintain a little more father-son contact during those fleeting years, I proposed to Dale, who was eight at the time, some evening sessions in radio (neither of us knew a cat's whisker from a rectifier). We started with a kit and diagrams for a simple set and worked on up to a complex one over a period of months. Son's elation sank to utter despair when he learned that we wouldn't be ready to move on in electronics and have a television built and operating by Thursday night in time for the Lone Ranger.

My wife and I weren't servants to our children, but we tried to be available when they needed us. Some of the best investments we ever made in energy expended or hours of sleep missed were when we talked out a girl-problem with one of them, or joked it up in the middle of the night on a family campout. Or when we encouraged them to keep working on an oration, term paper, Bible quiz, Little League baseball or any other legitimate interest. The boys came naturally by a certain amount of perseverance, and we wanted them to use it on everything they started! Dale admits that if he hadn't been so stubborn, he wouldn't have stuck it out in his first year in "med" school. We plead guilty to having contributed to his stubbornness. Upon his finishing internship I wrote to him (in part):

Your success as a doctor will derive not only from your skill and knowledge, but also from your sincere love for and interest in people. You will cure bodies, and your abilities are augmented by the love of God in your heart. Fortunately you inherited just enough Scotch tenacity to help pull you through the unbelievable hours of study and work. *I salute you, Dale.*

— With love from your proud Dad

- *To communicate with each boy at his own level, regularly and in depth; to keep the channels of rapport open between us.*

In *Arnold's Commentary,* I wrote a few years ago: "In our family of four sons there has been a minimum of trouble in the home. Analyzing this from the standpoint of several years' experience, I think it is probably due, in part at least, to the fact that my wife and I have always tried to draw the boys (or each other, as the case happened to be) into a conversational analysis of anything that seemed upsetting or disturbing, however large or small it might be. Many tensions died aborning when exposed to light and logic, and contributed valuable lessons on life as they expired."

Our family rapport really paid off when the boys were in college and developed some rather serious girl-problems. To one son I wrote (in part):

I recall that during the first several months of my association with the girl who is now your mother there were many times of despair because we didn't understand each other, and had no concept of the adjustments which had to be made to amalgamate two such gnarly personalities. Fortunately there was a deep inner attraction which held fast while we were filing and sandpapering ourselves and each other! . . . One of the things that helped us surmount three years of engagement 600 miles apart was the prayers we had together and separately for our relationship. . . . So your falling in love early may have its problems, but they are not insurmountable. The God-planned end of your situation may be marriage and physical union. And while our training says "wait" our 18-year-old bodies say "go!" It will require strength, determination, won't-power, and the grace of God for you to maintain the continual vigilance that is necessary. But it can be done.

One son now writes about our family rapport: "I treasured our child-parent relationship because it showed you were interested in what I was doing — kind of like having cheerleaders on the sidelines."

How the boys did like to catch their Dad or Mom doing or saying something stupid — especially after they got brave enough to laugh at us. Once after a chocolate cake had been served for supper, I cruised through the kitchen and seeing some leftover crumbs on the table, I scooped them up and ate them. Unbeknown to me, someone had just fixed the dog's supper there, and the crumbs were in fact

dog food. That brought a hearty round of laughter. And to a
man they remember something they call "Baa" candy, and
claim I was responsible for making it, and that term was
the actual family appraisal of how it tasted. Baa. Sherry is
famous for a statement made when traveling one summer.
While handing a root beer over the car seat to one of the
boys she said, "See how little of this you can keep from
spilling."

Some of these silly things were hard on our dignity, but
didn't hurt our family rapport one bit!

We didn't play up the "generation gap," or the "rebellious
teens or adolescence." With good rapport, we found it exciting to explore expanding horizons with our teenagers.

* *To enjoy family experiences and all of life together in as
many ways as possible. To deepen love in the family.*

The Bible says, "Husbands, love your wives." God might
be saying to parents, "Splash plenty of love around." In our
family activities, love took on many strange and wonderful
faces. Love was quality time spent with a child. Love was
Dad making cocoa to help celebrate someone's achievement. Love was campouts here and there and everywhere,
with hamburgers cooked and eaten in a rain-soaked tent.
Love was a treehouse with a fireman's pole for escape.
Love was a phrase that had its own special meaning, such
as "Now look here, McGee."

Love was a family hug when the boys came running to
join in. Love was talking quietly with a son about the death
of his grandmother. There was plenty of love in our home. It
showed. It captured Dad, Mom and the children — and carried over into their homes years later.

Recently I wrote:

I recall that when I was a teenager Dad and Mom
would sit on the piano bench together, singing their way
through the latest camp meeting songbook. Mother was
a soprano and Dad a bass, and never the twain did meet,
or come very close. That almost put the words to two
separate tunes, but they did start and end at the same
time. What they lacked in polish they made up in exuber-
ance. No doubt about it, it was contagious, and my

brother, sister, and I found ourselves going about singing the same songs.

So what could be more natural than family singing in my own home a generation later? We bought a church hymnal for each of us when all six of us were still together. We had our names imprinted on them, and kept them near the dining room table. Sunday noons after the meal we would select favorites and sing — to the improvement of both our digestions and our dispositions. "All Hail the Power of Jesus' Name" became a favorite, and "Crown Him Lord of All" became our family affirmation.

Eventually our at-home family got down to three: Sherry, Dan and me. One Sunday as we were shakily holding forth on some mighty hymn of the church, the front door of the house burst open and in paraded Dale and his family from Indianapolis, a hundred miles away. While we paused in the shock of surprise, he calmly announced: "We heard you singing, and thought you needed help!"

When any or all of our family comes together, it is almost spontaneous that songs of praises fill the air.*

- *To help each son to put together a framework of Christian responsibilities — for decision-making, problem solving and stewardship.*

"The last two to volunteer will help Mom with the dishes tonight." This challenge was tossed out to our four boys — and two eager-beavers hoping to escape said, "I will," and "I will!" From the other two, silence. Then it hit. The "escapees" were trapped — and we all had a good laugh at the unexpected turn of intentions.

One of the best examples of Christian responsibility I know was my father Dr. E.R. Benson of Westby, Wisconsin. When he found the Lord as his Savior, he patiently led his family until they too found Him. Dad went early to our little church every winter Sunday morning to build the fire; he was Sunday school superintendent and adult class teacher for as long as I can remember. Even during the depression,

---

* From *Light and Life*, (October 1975) Used by permission.

I never saw the offering basket go by without his putting something in it. Things of the world didn't interest him. He didn't buy a car until he absolutely had to and he bought no new clothes until Mom couldn't possibly repair his old ones. Somehow these demonstrations of Christian stewardship got through to a number of other people — notably his own family.

Years ago, my son Dale was accused of having driven past a stopped school bus. It was reported to the police and he had to appear before the Justice of the Peace to plead innocent or guilty. He told us in detail what happened, and had witnesses to verify it. He was not guilty, and pleaded thus before the Justice of the Peace, but had to post a $50 appearance bond. So then we had to engage an attorney and prepare to defend him in a trial. We waited and waited but the trial never came up and eventually the $50 came back to us in the mail. Dale recounts this time of testing as being proof of the confidence we had in his word.

Once when Dan had an experience that made me just furious (inside), I had to maintain a semblance of cool externally, hoping he would take the cue. Dan writes:

When I was disqualified from the Soap Box Derby, my little-boy self-centeredness could only let me see and feel *my* hurt. I didn't know that yours was probably deeper than mine, although thinking back on it now I can see how hard you tried to hide it, and how disappointed you were, that this horrendous thing had happened to your youngest son after so much anticipation. Looking back, that is one of my warmest, most compassionate memories — and I wish I had had the maturity to encourage *you* during that tough time.

The boys recently asked us how Sherry and I felt about some of the troublesome things they did.

One son spent a night in jail on a trumped-up charge of disturbing the peace while selling dictionaries in Texas. Among other things, this completely shattered his morale. Three sons were "campused" at college for one or another kind of rule infraction. One took a near-new car out on a date and before the evening was over the car was totaled and his girlfriend was in an intensive care ward.

How did we feel at these times? Deep concern because loved ones were hurting. But we also were praying fervently according to Romans 8:28 that the experience would not permanently scar the sensitivity and capabilities of those involved. Actually, these times helped to draw the family closer together, and closer to God.

All of the boys rate very highly the various times I spent with them privately. (Many of these little snatches of companionship I had almost forgotten.) Dan talks about the several times he and I went bowling together. All four sons remember fondly the days and weeks we worked together on various projects. One mentions the joys of joint discovery as we made prints in a photographic darkroom. Paul relates how he enjoyed "helping" me in my workshop and at the newspaper office when the other boys weren't around; our camaraderie on a missionary speaking trip, and the private talks on the "foibles" of females. Dale says he felt wonderful when he was singled out to stay with me for two days when the family was moving to Iowa from Texas; and recalls his pride as he and I took the trip together on the train, and also how he was impressed when I left my work and went with him to Akron for his derby race. Each boy and I learned to know each other pretty well.

They also claim that I am responsible for their acquiring several qualities: creativity, a sense of humor, a fun-loving disposition, shyness (introverted tendencies, such as they would rather be at home than at a party almost any time), adequate intelligence. And a few ideas: family is exciting and fulfilling; occupations can be rewarding; it is possible to change careers; firmness with love is a great combination; brainstorming is a productive way to solve problems.

But don't think I'm trying to say that all was perfect and peaceful. We were and are quite human, and had plenty of upsets and disappointments. Plans crumbled; schedules and wishes and boys and parents were in occasional conflict; some of our principles and regulations got bent out of shape and had to be revised, strengthened and straightened. We learned together, but at times we flubbed opportunities and missed them altogether. One son now relates: "I didn't acquire many of your talents; you and I were not 'buddies.' I was intimidated by your perfectionism. We had little or no common interest. And you vetoed my going out for the basketball team, even after the coach had invited me. Why?" (Same son also says re the above: "I was not adversely affected by any of these things — I actually became aware of them many years later!") Another son relates his wish that I had taught him some of my household and workshop skills. "But I wasn't brave enough to ask," he admits.

- *To handle discipline so (hopefully) the boys will know it is a part of life; that it is exercised in love; and is for the good of all the family.*

Sherry and I tried to run a "tight ship." We kept pretty close tab on where our sons were from the day they were born until they left for college — where, with whom, doing what, and when they were expected home. We provided space, indoor and outdoor activities, food, and encouraged them to bring their friends in. They did — and to this day the same friends still laugh with us about the "congregations" in our living room or the basketball games in our backyard.

The boys never had personal radios or record players. (We couldn't afford them.) Sherry and I provided a good hi-fi and lots of good records, and the boys played them at wall-shaking volume. Television programs to watch were chosen in family conference. We saw many good shows together, and the boys filled in with television sports when they couldn't be outside doing their own thing.

How did we handle run-of-the-mill discipline? Every which way. But largely we tried to be firm, flexible, and loving. We resorted to spankings when a series of misbehaviors couldn't otherwise be stopped, or when a situation came along that was sufficiently serious to require special emphasis — like the time two sons built a fire under a house in Texas. Minor squabbles between siblings we often let run their course, because it was easier on our nerves than getting emotionally involved in every little thing that came up.

The boys started early to use a great deal of ingenuity to circumvent parental restrictions so as to avoid possible punishments. Such as taking the cat to bed (strictly an undercover job), or smoothing over the frosting on a cake to conceal the disappearance of one fingerful, or holding back the Sunday school offering to gain a little more spending money for the week. The success of this type of activity at our house was extremely short-lived. They found to their dismay that both Mom and Dad were also children once, and had thought of and tried nearly all of those tricks.

There was something strange about the boys' hearing mechanisms. With the radio blaring and the baby crying, the faintest meow by the cat sent them running to the door to let her in. But when a firm parental summons was issued from the kitchen amid dishpan noises, the boys failed to hear it for several minutes, if at all. There must have been a secret antenna, located somewhere near the seat of wisdom; a bit of pants dusting usually improved reception.

Then there was the "apron-string-cutting." Our youngest when about six or seven years old, in great despair over something or other, announced one evening that next day after school he was going to run away from home. He didn't realize it, but he was already hacking away at the apron strings. The following morning at breakfast I casually mentioned that I had finally gotten all the parts and would start building a moon rocket, big enough for him to ride in, right after school that day. Needless to say, he and half a dozen of his friends were all lined up on the basement steps after school, and guess what I was doing right in front of them. Building a moon rocket. It took several such days; then came the outdoor tests; then the device won a prize in a Warsaw parade, and the subject of running away from home never came up again, at least not out loud. The apron strings held, temporarily.

Apron-string-cutting puts some parents into a state of shock and ties their discipline pattern into knots. It may start with a child making a simple request to do something special on his own, something not permitted up to that point. It could be a request for an extension of curfew time; or a request for a short absence from home; his own source of music and choice of volume level; or insistence on going away to college instead of staying home and attending the one in his own city; or it could be a sudden disinterest and skepticism about everything religious. Some adolescents are famous for testing out every precept they have accumulated thus far in their lives, and parents pray that what has been built into their characters and lives will be firm enough to hold.

*   *   *

Now, the dust has settled and quiet prevails. Worn hinges on the refrigerator have been repaired, and the food and clothing budgets have stabilized. One day Sherry said, "We're going to miss not having him around here." I did a double-take, and we had a good laugh over that idea. It showed how confused we were when our last youngster Dan left home for college!

In our family, from the very beginning, a Scripture verse pointed the way for all of us: *If any of you lacks wisdom, let him ask of God, who gives to all men generously* (James 1:5, NASB).

We did, and we received answers. We were given wisdom beyond ourselves. Problem solutions popped into our heads, or worked themselves out step-by-step. God used some of His choice people at critical times when we or the boys needed special help.

Sherry and I give thanks for every bit of family fun, accomplishment, victories small and great, spiritual growth, and lifelong usefulness that have evolved during the years we have been parents.

We joyfully attribute all blessings to our caring, loving heavenly Father.

One father is more than a hundred schoolmasters.
George Herbert

LYN AND RIK CRYDERMAN model Japanese kimonos for their parents and brothers on the family's return from missionary service.

W. Dale Cryderman

W. Dale Cryderman *is a newspaperman-turned-minister. His interests include cameras (he's a good photographer), airplanes (he's a pilot), and ham radios.*

Prior to his election to the office of bishop in the Free Methodist Church, he served as a conference superintendent, a Youth For Christ director over Japan and Korea, and a regional youth director in his own denomination.

The Cryderman's first son William is an ordained minister of the Free Methodist Church. He is a member of the American Guild of Organists and has incorporated his musical talents into his ministry. He and his wife Sharon serve their church in Dearborn, Michigan.

Dale, their second son, heads a high school science department in Brooklyn, Michigan, where he also serves as town clerk. His wife Elizabeth is Brooklyn's assistant librarian.

Their third son, Lyn, is a teacher of English literature at his alma mater, Spring Arbor College in Michigan. Esther, his wife, has done the illustrations for three Y.M.C.A. books.

Richard — or "Rik" as he is known to his friends — is the youngest of the Cryderman boys. He, his wife Kristin, and their three children, occupy the parsonage of the Albion, Michigan Free Methodist Church, the same congregation his parents served a generation earlier.

Dale and Dorothy Cryderman live in Winona Lake, Indiana. Although separated from their children by a couple of hundred miles, they nevertheless keep in touch. They've discovered that ham radio is "the next best thing to being there."

My preparation for "fathering" began under the tutelage of a great Dad whom I had for only fifteen years. His name was William. He was a carpenter by trade and his specialty was cabinetmaking. He entered the ministry at the age of thirty-five following the steps of his own father who was a lay minister.

Life had not been particularly kind to him. Like many of his generation, demands for family survival limited his education. Then I, his only son, at three years of age, became the victim of tuberculosis in the knee. Shortly after that my mother spent twelve months in a TB sanitarium outside Detroit.

I recall his telling me of his determination that I should participate in my first Sunday School Christmas program and how he made crutches for me so I could go up on the platform and recite my poem of the Nativity.

It was his strong arms that gave me strength and comfort for the many trips to the hospital. His hands carefully massaged and manipulated my knee following heat treatments in a special oven he had made. In spite of my mother's protests he encouraged me to play baseball, even though it meant running bases on crutches and always having to be the catcher. He repudiated any idea that his son was a cripple, even turning his back when I fell in order that I would learn to get up on my own.

In the North Michigan forests he taught me to aim a rifle, to hear sounds of animals, to follow a trout stream and to camp out. But, better yet, in the home and from the pulpit, I learned how exciting the Christian life could be and good Christian people are. I learned on my own about the imperfections of church members; but never from the lips of my father.

In my teens we shared the same hospital room for the last months of his life. We entered the same day, father and son, with the dreaded TB. In those months he shared spiritual lessons with me. I learned of the reality of God, the dependability of His Word, the inevitability of times of testing, and the triumph of truth. For even as the doctor gave him the news of the certainty of his death in a few weeks, he said with confidence: *For to me, to live is Christ, and to die is gain* (Phil. 1:21, NASB).

*   *   *

Church bells were ringing that December morning in 1936 when the doctor proudly announced: "You are the father of a 9 lb. 10 oz. boy. Dorothy is just fine." But, back of this had been long hours of suffering and complications and the solemn warning: "I'm not sure we can save either Dorothy or the baby." How alone I felt. And I was. I had turned my back on God and the church in rebellion. I had rationalized that God had been unfair to me in snatching my father away when I needed him so much. A loving God wouldn't leave my mother and me homeless in the depths of depression days.

Now things were better — but I was a father. Frightened, without resources, and with only fifteen years of memories of what a father was like, the task was too big. But less than a month after William Leon (Bill) had arrived, Dorothy and I turned our lives over to God and accepted Christ as our Lord and Savior. Now I felt possibly I could make it, if God would just make me like my Dad.

Excitement reigned in those first months. We weighed our firstborn every day and charted his progress. If he had the sniffles we phoned the doctor frantically for advice. Colic was a major disaster. As we walked the floor, we prayed earnestly and were very sure God had never heard petitions like ours before. He never chided us nor let us know how many prayers from new parents He heard every hour.

Our family grew until we had four boys. Bill was followed by Dale in 1942, then seven years later came Lyn, followed by Rik in thirteen months. Four distinct personalities to try the patience of a Job and the wisdom of a Solomon, qualities woefully lacking in the father of the home. We experimented on Bill, made corrections in procedures on Dale, then started all over again on Lyn, only to be interrupted by Rik making his appearance. By the time Rik arrived we had capable babysitters in Bill and Dale. For twenty-five years we had boys in school. We became experts in PTA, band concerts, dramatics, musicales, football, basketball, track and cross-country. We had been to so many parent-teacher consultations that we felt more like consultants than parents.

School and its related activities were important. We encouraged participation in a broad range of activities, but kept reminding the boys that their deportment at school was important.

"If you get in trouble at school, you will *really* be in trouble at home," we repeatedly reminded them.

We stood with the teachers in their important role of molding the lives of our sons. Only once did we side with one of the boys against a teacher whom we felt had been unfair. Not too bad a record when you consider the number of teachers over the long span of years.

But back to the birth of our first son Bill. I could see early reflections of myself and our family as I looked at him. His blue eyes were very much like mine and my grandfather's. His hair was blond like mine at that time (later he showed similar signs of baldness characterizing his father today). And his name, William, was the first name of both his grandfather and father. But more important, he was a Cryderman, and I had been the last of the Crydermans in my father's branch of the family. I had contributed nothing to the value of that name, but was very conscious that it was a good name. The two generations I knew had made it so.

Grandfather William Cryderman was a big, genial, loving personality who raised a family of four children and served as one of the pioneer lay pastors in the Free Methodist Church in Northern Michigan. One of these pastorates was a two-point circuit with the churches separated by more than one hundred miles. People who knew him loved him, although my memories of him are vague. He died when I was very young. But I can remember the twinkle of his blue eyes as he romped with me and I knew he loved me.

My own father had contributed much to the name. He was hardworking, dedicated, intensely loyal to his church, a self-made student of the Word. He was a joyful Christian who touched hundreds of lives. He made every church he served more conscious of the need for reaching out with the Gospel of the Lord Jesus Christ. While serving a church, he always had additional preaching points where he discovered responsive people. Young people loved him and were drawn to him. Respected by both saint and sinner, he was the living expression of God's love. Could I pass on to my family the value of the name? That became one of my goals as a father.

"We own nothing more valuable than our name Cryderman," I told the boys as they were growing up. As far as I knew it had never been tainted by hypocrisy, nor disgraced by immorality, nor embarrassed by lack of integrity. We owed it to ourselves and to past generations to preserve the good name. It might never be famous, nor outstanding, but I felt its quality must always be preserved. Could I pass on the same concept to my sons? I tried.

*   *   *

Respect may appear to be a very small and ordinary thing, but its ramifications are great. We began early in the lives of our children to teach respect for the Bible. It was never to be covered by any other book or magazine when it lay on the coffee table or desk. It was always to be prominent. It was God's Word. From respect it was easy to move on to memorization and use of the special book.

And in an attempt to teach respect for God's house we encouraged each of the boys to follow the scripture readings on Sunday morning and to outline the message. This also served as a means of maintaining reverence. My invalid grandmother had taught me to do this years before so I could share my father's messages with her. It wasn't long until we had outlines of sermons by bishops, evangelists, missionaries, and of course my messages were there too.

Just recently an eleven-year-old grandson visited us and attended morning worship. After the service he showed me his outline of Pastor Mauer's message on the Church. Three generations of sermon outliners have come from respect.

Perhaps it was because their father had fought so many physical battles up to mid-way in high school that respect for others, particularly the handicapped or the poor, became a high priority. I had been the skinniest kid on the block, the last chosen for a pickup game, and the one left out because of a lame knee and later almost socially ostracized because of my bout with tuberculosis. I was determined my boys would be friends of the underdog.

As they progressed through school each had his own expertise — basketball, football, track, music, science or art. But they were never allowed to develop attitudes of superiority over peers less talented. Each had close friends among the less privileged. We frequently heard stories of how they had come to the defense of others.

Probably one of my most glaring weaknesses was being too "authoritarian" in demanding this respect in the home. I know better now that respect is something earned, not demanded.

However, it was made clear that their mother must be the most respected one on the family roster. She was their confidant, especially if they felt I had been unfair. But she always stood firm when it came to family standards and expectations while occasionally weakening when she knew Dad had exceeded normal levels of firmness.

My lowest moments came when one of the boys would succumb to peer pressure (or satanic power) and violate the family standards. There was the day when an eleven-year-old came home reeking with tobacco. In our confrontation, he had no answers. Who have you been with? What have you been doing? Other questions, still no answers. Dad moved into action with a spanking which grew more severe as the stubborn silence persisted. Finally, the obvious: "Jerry and I were smoking." Then the emotional dam broke and tears of sorrow flowed freely.

I have never been proud of that scene. Particularly when in later years it was referred to as "the time Dad beat the tar out of me." I will admit to being too severe, but after seeing my father die with TB and remembering my own bout with the disease, my tolerance was very low to anything that would weaken the lungs. Add to this the vivid memories of how our family had been disrupted when my mother spent a whole year in the sanitarium when I was only six years old.

How did we handle those moments when I was too severe? Sometimes it was what our youngest son Rik called "family powwows" where I would admit I had been too severe and feelings were patched up. Other times (I am told now by grown sons), "You would turn around and do something with us that we particularly enjoyed and we knew you weren't mad at us as persons; but disappointed at our actions."

*   *   *

My wife had most of the responsibility for Bill and Dale who were six years apart. She had to be both mother and father. My work as a regional director of our denominational youth organization kept me on the road five weeks out of six. Since my time with the boys was limited it had to be quality time. We packed that one week full of father and son and family activities. But Dorothy was there caring for them and training them all the time.

One day when they were high school students, the level of kidding their mother rose higher and higher until it appeared to me it was about to get out of hand. I broke in with the statement: "Look guys, you may be able to get away with that with your mother; but I won't allow you to talk that way to my wife." They soon discovered the difference between "Mom" and "Dad's wife," who deserved special respect.

In spite of my weaknesses, the measure of our relationships as a family would rate on the high side. Sometimes evidence of the "father and son relation" took on ridiculous forms. Such as the following Father's Day letter from Bill when he was a senior at Hillside College:

Hello you old bat:

Since this is just about Father's Day I guess I have to get you something.

Even tho we fight and everything I still think you're a swell guy. Thanks for you and mom having me. I couldn't have picked a better family.

Last week it made me feel good to have people say they had heard three generations of Crydermans preach. I think if the Lord lets me be half as successful as you have been I'll be thankful.

I know I'll never forget "my Dad" you know, like when I need a loan or something. Ha.

Well, I hope the Lord blesses you a whole lot for about fifty more years.

This letter may sound sentimental; but it's a whole lot cheaper than a card.

Your eldest son,
Bill

The atmosphere of home for four growing boys was very important to us. We never had large salaries and couldn't afford many of the things that some people think are necessary for happiness and fulfillment, so we had to concentrate on priorities.

But we felt we could not afford to raise our family without surrounding them with certain cultural benefits. We couldn't afford not to have good books, magazines and high quality record albums. Could these have played a part in developing two ministers, a high school science teacher and an English professor in a Christian college?

One of the standards for the family was that if you went out for sports you had to balance it with participation in the arts. No athletic bums around our house. Sports by all means, but also choir and band, organ and piano, drama and art. We gave in on this principle only once when a Christian college would not allow participation in both sports and music. Our reasoning was we wanted life-long activities and viewed participation in sports as of short duration. No, it wasn't easy! Repetitive exercises on the piano; weird sounds from a voice student, and a beginner on the trumpet did not make for a peaceful environment, especially when all this was going on at the same time. Then add to that, the visual chaos of an easel and splotches of oil paints in the corner of the family room.

Many nights the tranquility of the household was disturbed by an athletic team barging in and one of the boys awakening his mom with the plaintive message: "We're back home from the game; but there is no place open where we can get something to eat." Soon Mom had hamburgers frying, french fries sizzling and hot chocolate bubbling for a roomful of hungry fellows.

The other side of the coin of "atmosphere" is that everyone in the family is a part of it. Each one of us had a role to fill and how we played determined the home's atmosphere. This meant everyone had a job too. Household chores were divided and printed copies were given to each boy. Everyone had to take a turn doing dishes, running the sweeper, helping with cooking, doing the laundry and even washing windows. Each was responsible for taking care of his room and making his own bed daily.

Any problems? Yes, but in working them through we worked out relational problems at the same time. Occasionally one of the boys would feel he had been given too long a work list. Their mother was both judge and jury and carefully meted out justice (or was it injustice?). Sometimes feelings were hurt in the distress of what appeared to be unfairness. I would come up with an old family verse that many times turned tears to laughter. I had learned it from my father and it went like this:

> Poor Jocko,
> Dida man giva red hota penny?
> Maka feela bad?
> Never mind, Jocko
> Giva nice peanut,
> Maka feela good again.

Corny? Absolutely. But I remembered my father using it on me, so I passed it on, and now we all laugh about its therapeutic value, even though the days of organ grinders with monkeys have disappeared.

Learning to manage money became an exercise in negotiation and responsibility. There wasn't much money when Bill and Dale were growing up so I can't remember many details about how we handled them. But things were a bit different when Lyn and Rik were in high school, so one day we sat down to figure out how much money they needed each month. Haircuts, school lunches, high school activities and all expenses were figured in. Then Dad drew up a legal contract providing a certain amount of money and in return the boys were to do the yard work, take care of the cleaning of their own rooms, wash the car, help their mother in certain chores and look after "KoKo" the dog. Signatures were officially affixed and the contract was in effect. It worked.

School lunches were not particularly enjoyed so they conned their mother into putting up their lunches and discovered they had extra spending money. Come to think about it, whose side was she on anyway?

Although rules and regulations were few, delay in obedience was not tolerated. If there was any hesitation Dad or Mom would start to count — one, two, three — when the boys were small. Usually before we got to three action was under way. As they matured the counting was discarded. We knew we could depend upon them to give immediate obedience.

Because I was away so much the boys were taught that, without any exception, Mother must know where they were at all times. Changes in plans for an evening were acceptable, providing a phone call was made to inform Mom.

During their dating years we lived in a college town, Spring Arbor, Michigan, and the time to be home at night coincided with college standards. An unwritten law was that their dates were to be brought by the house to be introduced to their parents.

Cars were no big problem. We just insisted that ownership be delayed until after graduation from high school. Dad's car could be borrowed as long as they maintained one hundred dollars in savings to cover the deductable in case of an accident. Fortunately there was never a need to use it, for they were all good drivers.

It was a variety of many different things that made our father-son relations meaningful and brought us close together. Soon after each one had finished his driver's training classes, I gave him the opportunity to act as my chauffeur on long business trips. These presented quality times for talking together without interruption or competition. Even prolonged times of silence were respected and appreciated for meaningful fellowship.

Annual deer hunting trips in Northern Michigan were ideal for spending time together in the outdoors, either to be enjoyed or endured, dependent upon the measure of devotion to the sport. Hunting actually was incidental. We were out in the woods before daylight, hiking for miles over snow-covered trails, sitting quietly on runways, enjoying or enduring the cold and snow but always looking forward to noon. That was the hilarious time, cooking over an open fire, and roaring with laughter over some incident, like the time someone had sat in the dim light of dawn staring at what he thought was a big buck, only to discover it was a weird-shaped stump.

Practical jokes were saved an entire year to be played on me during deer hunting. One of the better ones was the year we camped in our travel trailer. I informed them that being the oldest of the group and the father, I should have the electric blanket. After getting comfortably tucked in for the night, I started getting warmer and warmer until I rose up and shouted: "Let's open some windows, I can't stand the heat." Then, gales of laughter. Dale, on the floor in a sleeping bag, had been turning the controls of my blanket higher and higher while all waited for my reaction.

Laughing at Dad seemed a normal pastime in our family. Even yet they remind me of when we got our first riding mower which I promptly started up and rode into the pond at the back of our lot, all because I failed to discover where the brakes were. Mechanics just was not one of my specialties.

Then there were the serious moments that brought us together. In all of my travels at home and overseas, the family knew that any sickness or accident would bring me promptly to their side. My priorities were established early: God would be first, my wife second, my sons third, and then my work. I have never been sorry or tempted to change the order of those priorities.

Could we ever forget an ambulance ride in the middle of the night, taking Bill to an army hospital in Korea? He had been traveling with the Venture for Victory basketball team and picked up a serious infection. For several days we were together, away from the rest of the family, but secure in a growing faith that God was with us in the midst of a serious dilemma.

We returned to Japan only to have another hospital experience. This time Bill had appendicitis and we were at the mercy of a doctor who spoke no English. Surgery performed in the middle of the night was followed by gangrene. We suffered with Bill those next days as we watched him lose both weight and strength. One early morning about four o'clock, while spending the entire night with him, I stepped outside his room searching the Scriptures for assurance. I found what I needed as I read the thirty-second chapter of Jeremiah: "Behold, I am the Lord, the God of all flesh: Is there anything too hard for me?" And then in the next chapter I read: "Call unto me, and I will answer thee, and show thee great and mighty things, which thou knowest not."

There were similar hospital experiences with Dale and Lyn while they were in their teens. Praying together and sharing together in these times of crisis brought us into a close relationship that was to last.

As superintendent of a growing conference with demands upon my time that took me away from so many family events, God had a lesson to teach me through our youngest son. Rik simply asked, "Dad will you be home Friday night when we put on the class play?" I checked my schedule and told him I had an out-ot-town meeting. His reply cut like a knife. "Dad, you're never around when important things happen."

Right then I made a change in procedure. I wrote in my schedule all the dates of the boys' activities. It took a bit of adjusting but I was there with their mother for cross-country meets as we cheered them on. We made it to the football and basketball games. We sat through plays and concerts — and felt the richer for it.

The family vacation was always the highlight of the year. Sometimes it was a trip to Florida for unforgettable days with Grandma. Other times it was to North Michigan for fishing, hunting and canoe trips down the fast-flowing rivers. Miles of travel were spent in games involving finding the letters of the alphabet, counting horses, only to bury them when you passed a cemetery on your side of the highway — and singing. It was in the car that the boys learned to sing parts so that eventually we had three and then four-part harmony. We roared with laughter as we tried to imitate male quartets singing the "Stone Song." And became meditative as we would sing, "Oh to be Like Thee, Blessed Redeemer."

We had much valuable help from the church in the raising of our family. There was Mama Roney, who brought her girls Sandy and Delores to stay overnight on those rare occasions when both Dorothy and I had to be away. The older boys spent many happy Sunday afternoons with them.

Uncle Al and Aunt Ruth had so many pretty things. Often on Sunday evening after the services, we'd go there to relax and enjoy the beauty of their home. Dale still remembers a trip to Chicago at Christmas time when Uncle Al took him to have his picture taken with Santa Claus. And there was Jinny, who baby-sat for the little ones.

The list would have to include Uncle Dick and Aunt Betty; Auntie Vie and Uncle Dick who lived next door, and Uncle Jake and Aunt Cora. Then there was Aunt Nettie whose prayers with the boys, and for them, added a spiritual dimension to their lives. During college days there was Uncle Dunk and Aunt Bernie who took a very special interest in the boys who now were growing into manhood. It was Uncle Dunk who patiently listened to their problems and counseled them.

Lyn and Rik will never forget packets of pencils from golf courses and paper match folders for Rik's collection from all over the world given to them by Mrs. Hugh White. Caring people — scores of them — added something to the lives of my boys by way of their friendship, interest and example that could not be duplicated in any other way.

Religious training began early and just seemed to be a normal part of their lives. Bible stories, gospel songs, table graces, family devotions and parental prayers with them at bedtime, combined into a meaningful routine.

One morning at family devotions, when we usually sang a hymn, Billy, about three, asked, "Daddy, could we sing the "fill me up" song?" While I puzzled over what he meant he began the tune to the hymn: "Fill me now, fill me now, Jesus come and fill me now." It was one of those mornings I needed the "filling up" of Christ's presence and felt that Billy had done no harm to the meaning of the hymn.

Among church activities the annual Family Camp Meeting played a big part in our spiritual development. One year when Lyn was about six he came home from the camp Bible school to share with us that he had gone forward and asked Jesus to come into his heart. The next day he reported again that he had gone forward and the next day, and again the next. About that time I thought I should explain it was not necessary to go forward each day to keep saved. He looked up with such sincerity and said, "But daddy, it makes me feel so good." I decided to postpone further theological training. I didn't want him to have a religion that was only "feeling," but I definitely wanted him to have a religious experience that included feeling.

There were struggles. Each son was a normal growing boy with temptations; with weaknesses as well as strengths. We remember well the night Bill came to our bedroom in Tokyo to talk about his problems, and telling him that as much as we loved him as parents we couldn't make his decisions for him. He went back to his room to pray and to settle some things knowing that while his parents cared, it was up to him to enter into a personal relationship with Christ.

Another time when one of the boys had gone away with friends not very well known to us, Dorothy and I were awakened out of a sound sleep with a burden to pray. We both felt the same, that trouble was brewing and Satan was at work. How long we spent in prayer I do not remember but the next day we received word of how God had delivered us from a disastrous situation.

Another time in an early romance, one of the boys was becoming quite serious with a girl. We questioned whether she was the one for him, but to talk about it would have had a reverse effect. So we just prayed and committed it to the Lord. Our prayers were answered, the breakup was traumatic, but our son knew the will of God. Soon after, he began dating the girl who later became his wife.

Speaking of dating and marriage, we did have moments of trying to make what we thought would be an ideal match, only to hear: "Oh, Dad, did you ever try to hold hands with your sister?" The girl, in this case, seemed perfect, but they had grown up with a brother-sister relationship. Romance was out of the question.

In spite of our failures at the one and only attempt at matchmaking, each boy made a better choice than we could have. We never accepted daughters-in-law, but daughters! Can you imagine the joy of four daughters after raising four sons?

Sharon, steady in her Christian experience, was just right for Bill. Liz, who came from Scotland and met Dale at Spring Arbor College, brought the talents and gifts that made Dale complete. Esther, a Baptist, raised by strict, conservative parents who came to the States from Germany just before her birth, was ideal for Lyn. And, Kris, a Free Methodist preacher's daughter, whom Rik knew from conference activities, was the partner God had for him in the ministry.

* * *

Close relationships as a family have paid off as, repeatedly, we have all dropped what we were doing and come to the help of each other.

In 1971 Dorothy and I were in a serious automobile accident just outside Spring Arbor. Both of us suffered painful injuries. The car was totaled after a tree fell on us in a freak wind storm as we traveled down the highway. The ambulance had barely arrived at the hospital when all four boys converged on the scene. They moved back and forth between us in the emergency room and in X-ray, praying, encouraging and doling out good-natured kidding over our predicament.

Pain-filled days in the hospital, where we both suffered from concussions and neck and back injuries, were made easier by their frequent visits and telephone calls. Upon our release, Rik and Kris moved in and took over the management of the home.

Christmas came that year just six days after we were released from the hospital and will never be forgotten. Grandson Brent, age four, recited the entire Christmas story from the scriptures. Dale had scraped up bits of broken glass from the demolished car and made a motto which read: "His Will — My Peace."

I had written an essay, "Christmas Came Early This Year," which I planned to read, but emotions overcame me. Lyn, the stalwart athlete, said he would read it, but only made it through a few lines. It made the rounds of each of the boys until someone had regained enough composure to complete it. It was simple, but from the heart, and may have been induced by medication — I'll leave that for someone else to judge. But this is the way it went:

Our Christmas arrived early this year. Actually, it arrived on December 10th at 1:30 p.m. Heavy dark clouds churned in the sky overhead and tornadic winds whipped huge trees into fierce gyrations on a rampage, while we traveled comfortably in the new Buick.

Suddenly, a resounding crash, a quick stop without touching the brakes, flying glass, a ripping of metal, and chaos broke our tranquility as rapidly as a bolt of lightning flashing in a summer sky.

Quiet, suppressed moans came from out of nowhere, arousing me from unconsciousness, and forced frantic gropings for my dearest who authored those sobs. Then it came clear, the roof of the car had been smashed down upon us as a huge portion of a tree had fallen and wrapped its clutches around us as if to demand our lives.

Then it came — our 1971 Christmas present, quietly, miraculously, and definitely — the gift of life! Pain, bleeding wounds, concussions, and torn muscles — but, there it was, sweet, real, beautiful, life. Ours from the Giver of Life. It was delivered personally by Him, there in the wreckage, and as He stayed close by us in sterile hospital rooms. Rooms where faithful nurses and a most efficient doctor cared for our needs.

So on Christmas eve, 1971, children, grandchildren, friends, neighbors and all around us are beautiful, for you see we received our Christmas present early on December 10th at 1:30 p.m.

If I could try fathering again, would I do anything different? Yes, more things than I can enumerate. Writing this chapter I have relived the pain of impatience, felt the hot tears of having corrected in anger, the loneliness of having been too busy and the ache of missing golden opportunities of sharing.

But basic things like respect, family life, church, striving for excellence, I would emphasize again. Only better, now that I have added to fathering — grandfathering.

Diogenes struck the father when the son swore.
Burton

PAUL AND DELORIS ELLIS with their three sons and their families, pause for the photographer outside of church.

Paul N. Ellis

Paul N. Ellis, *whose shock of white hair frames an alert and handsome face, has never believed that when you come into the church you must park your brains outside. A dedicated churchman with a keen mind, he has invested forty-five years in Christian ministry, the last fifteen in the bishopric. Across those years he has brought his considerable personal force to focus on whatever task he has attempted to do.*

He and his wife Deloris have raised three sons, all churchmen, who show the same regard for the life of the mind. All three hold master's degrees in their chosen fields.

John is a mechanical engineer and a supervisor in research and development in Bell Laboratories, Holmdel, New Jersey. He and his wife Shirley live with their family in Freehold, nearby.

Stanley and his wife Jolene live in Indianapolis where he is a junior high school teacher, head of the social science department, and coach of a cross-country team.

Charles is the director of special education in an educational cooperative that encompasses four school districts in Marion County, Indiana. He and Joanne also live in Indianapolis.

The senior Ellises, grandparents of nine, live in Winona Lake, Indiana. Although Paul Ellis regards highly the trust his church has shown him in electing him to the bishopric, he says, "My deepest satisfaction, aside from the great gift of God's grace, comes from my marriage and parenting role."

"Dad, how did you and Mom do it?"

Our second son Stan stood in the hall peering into my study. He and his wife Jolene were visiting us and he had just put his ten-months-old son Curt to bed. Stan looked as if the weight of the world had settled on his shoulders.

"I mean it," he said, his gray eyes serious, as he came into the room and sat down. "This little fellow of ours confronts me with my greatest challenge. I'd like to know how I can raise my son to become a man like John and Chuck, and, yes, even me. I have to admit you and Mom have done very well."

And I had to admit to some sanctified pride just then!

It's true. Our three sons, now men aged between thirty-six and forty-two, are something special. You'd expect a father to say so, I know, but you might also expect a modest man to be a bit less open about it. Yet these men are persons I would admire sincerely if they belonged to another family. In fact, I know many others just like them whom I do admire in the same way.

John is our eldest. He has three college and university degrees and works professionally as a supervising engineer in research and development for Bell Laboratories of the American Telephone and Telegraph Company near his home in Freehold, New Jersey. He is married to Shirley, a lovely Canadian girl whose parents have been dear friends of ours. They have three teenage children who are active Christian young people. John has served in many positions of lay leadership in the Free Methodist Church and is as concerned as a pastor with its spiritual progress.

Stan is fourteen months younger than John. He too is professionally settled in a vocation to which he believes God has called him. He's the head of the social sciences department in a large junior high school, and is a track coach. He met his wife Jolene at Greenville College, a Christian school in Illinois. She had been converted through Youth for Christ. They have two children now in their teens, a son and a daughter, both members of the church. Stan holds a master's degree in counseling from Indiana University and has made a ministry to youth out of his teaching opportunities.

Chuck, at thirty-six, is our youngest. He married Joanne, the granddaughter of a man who gave me my first employment as a student. They met and fell in love when she was a freshman and he a senior at Greenville College, and married soon after his graduation. He holds the master's degree with a certification in special education. He is director of the special education program in four school districts of Marion County.

He and Joanne have four children; the oldest are twin sons nine years old; the youngest a little girl who looks like her mother, with a lively son in between. Chuck and Joanne are active in a young congregation in Indianapolis, a church all three of our boys helped to found just ten years ago.

I suppose I could wish that one of them had followed me into the Christian ministry as a pastor, but I couldn't desire them to be any more faithful to Christ and committed to the church than they are. John put it right one day when the four of us were playing golf. I asked, with some pretention of seriousness, "How does it happen none of you fellows entered the ministry?" With a light blow to my shoulder John responded, "Dad, we're going to be the kind of laymen you've always wanted!"

On this evening Stan's question about raising his son called my attention to how fortunate we really are. My thoughts ran back across the years and I remembered these men as little fellows growing up in our home. I recalled some of the difficult times in the years of high school and college. I was reminded that some of my dearest friends, my peers in age and cultural advantages, have been grievously disappointed in their children. How did it happen so well with us?

It requires greater temerity than I possess to try to answer Stan's question. Only the childless or the doctrinaire come up with glib words about success in raising children. My immediate reply to Stan was like that of the milkman in *Fiddler On the Roof*. When he was asked where the Jewish community gets its tradition, he said: "I'll tell you. I don't know."

Were we just lucky? Sometimes I almost think so. My wife Deloris once overheard a woman in a drugstore turn down the suggestion of the clerk that she buy a lottery ticket. She chuckled and responded pleasantly, "Oh, no. I never gamble. I've never been lucky — except when I met and married my husband!"

My wife liked that and claims she feels the same way.

But we know that it's much more than luck when you build a happy marriage and establish a sound Christian home. In fact, Deloris and I were brought together by a most unusual providence. I had just finished my first year in a community college when my father decided it would be best to move to a city where I could attend university. We were poor. My only hope of higher education appeared to depend on being able to live at home while attending school.

With that in mind, my father requested a reassignment as a pastor. He asked the superintendent of the district if he might be sent to a church where I could go to school. The superintendent agreed readily. The church at Bloomington, Indiana, needed a pastor and Indiana University would give me the opportunity to major in mathematics as I desired. But when the appointments were read by the bishop, Dad was sent to Danville, Illinois! The pastor who was appointed to Bloomington was as surprised and disappointed as my father. The superintendent had forgotten and the bishop didn't know. We moved to Danville and I went broke over the next several years trying to get my education.

But at Danville I met Deloris!

Deloris Wells had been converted out of a modern pagan home. When I returned from college I found her working with my mother in the youth program of the church. She was a radiant, mature Christian, talented, lively and interesting. She soon became my best friend as we worked together. And when I thought of marriage I decided I should marry my best friend! If God can use the forgetfulness of a well-meaning superintendent to bring together two persons who have been so happy across these years, then I can trust the providence of God.

We know that we also have had God's help in the life of our family. From the beginning, when our first child was coming, we prayed daily for the young life forming so wondrously within Deloris. As we joyfully shared the mystery of physical generation, we talked of the wonder of creation and the greatness of God. We asked God to take our child and to work His will in the life yet to be born.

God gave me a great wife. Deloris was so steady, so confident of God, so courageous, that somehow I believed I could be a good father too! Her love has been so strong and consistent that all of her four men (we didn't have the joy of another lady in our home) have learned how to love in the same way. Deloris has never pretended or put on airs, to my knowledge, nor has she pushed to produce over-achievers in her three sons or husband. She has been confident of her own worth because Christ died for her, and has accepted each of us on the same terms. Such a mother (and wife) relieves some of the pressures so common in our competitive society. My sons were fortunate in the mother God gave them.

That evening as Stan and I talked he answered his own question: "I believe the most important thing is love. I always knew you and Mom loved us, in spite of everything."

"I can illustrate," Stan continued. "In my third year in Riverdale (the high school he attended in Toronto) Frankie and the other fellows I ran with began to experiment with sex. They had dates with girls from school. They'd meet during the warm afternoons along the banks of the Don River. They told me of making out under the trees in secluded corners of the park."

I remembered Frankie. How I had feared his influence on Stan.

"Well, one afternoon," Stan said seriously, "the fellows made a date for me. They urged me to go with them. I remember how tempted I was."

He paused. I had talked with my sons about sex. Within the family circle we had projected films to instruct and inspire them to chastity, and we encouraged them to ask questions. I had told them they would some day marry — that they'd want a girl who could come to them in marriage without sordid, compromising memories to disturb and embarrass, and that they should consider it just as important for them to go to the marriage altar without illicit sexual experiences to haunt them. I knew of course that they were responsible for their decisions. As a parent I couldn't go with my children into all the varied places where temptation could assault.

"Then I thought of Mother and you," Stan said. "I knew how disappointed you'd be if I did what the fellows were suggesting. So I said, 'No. You fellows are fools.' And I came on home."

Nothing is stronger than love, we agreed that evening. But how do we make love an effective force in the family?

The basic requirement I'm sure, is that love be sincere. Parents must be committed to their children at a level as deep as religious commitment. It isn't necessary that every child be the result of the considered choice of the parents through family planning. But when the mother knows she's pregnant, both father and mother must then give genuine love and commitment to the unfolding life in their midst. A young pastor, in his first sermon to his new congregation, said: "Now don't expect me to love you immediately. Give me time." Our eldest son, who heard of it, said: "Dad, the pastor should have loved those people from the moment the bishop assigned him to serve them!" So it should be with parents. The emotions may be tardy and varied but love is a commitment to responsibility and loyalty.

Love must be shown. A child must know he's loved. "Poor Judd," according to the lyric in *Oklahoma*, loved his fellowmen, but "he never let on . . . so nobody ever knowed it!" Some people are more articulate than others but there are many ways to express love, and we can let each other know of our caring, if we will.

Love's expectations must be clear in a father's leadership. I agree with those who say we must love our children unconditionally. It doesn't follow, however, that there should be no expectations clearly defined to our children. Stan knew that sexual immorality would defile him and deeply hurt his parents. It was love and knowledge that constrained him.

John had learned at the age of six that stealing could never be acceptable. He came home from the neighborhood store with a handful of potato chips he'd lifted from an open box on the counter.

"Look what I snitched from old man Farlow," he cried gleefully as he showed his mother.

Everyone (father, brother, and Mr. Farlow) was impressed by the restitution that followed. It wasn't easy, but there was nothing to do but return to the store with money to pay for the chips. John learned then and there.

I recall John's confidence when he began going out with girl friends. The day of his first date I asked him: "John, would you like any suggestions on how to treat your friend this evening?"

"I don't think so, Dad," he replied. "I've taken Mother into town many times."

Later, on his wedding day, an older friend waggishly asked if he could give John any last minute instructions.

"I don't need your help," he laughed. "Dad's taught me all I need to know."

That couldn't have been absolutely true, of course, but we have good reason to believe our sons knew we loved them. They knew also what we expected of them.

My experiences as a father have shown me that love at its highest and best rises from strong Christian faith, and that family love should be the reflection of the self-giving love of "the God and Father of our Lord Jesus Christ."

As far back as I can trace our family, religious faith has been strong and demanding. My great-grandfather was a country doctor in southern Indiana. He served two counties and made house calls by horse and buggy. Through long days and nights of rugged travel and demanding work he witnessed to his faith and his love of God and man.

My grandfather, John Martin Ellis, was a farmer who served church and community as songmaster for many years. I've heard him, when he was in his middle eighties, lift his voice in song during a time of testimony, praise and worship. His clear tone and radiant face caused great rejoicing as he sang: "When they ring those golden bells for you and me!"

The grandfather of our sons, the Rev. O.P. Ellis, gave more than forty years to the ministry of the church as evangelist, missionary and pastor.

Neither I nor our sons can remember a time when prayer was not an integral part of family life. The practice continues to this day in their homes as well. God is real to us all. We believe He knows us and sees us. We believe He loves us, not because we're worthy, but because He's gracious. To paraphrase a common motto, "God loves us and we love one another."

I don't wish to imply that religion has been taken for granted. We've refused to accept formal compliance or legalistic morality for the real stuff of Christian discipleship. On the other hand, we did not exclude our sons from identification with and activity in the religious life of our home or the church. We felt no obligation to hold them off until they had need of an *adult* conversion of some kind after the bitterness of immorality and alienation.

In keeping with my conviction regarding family religion, we brought each son in turn to the baptismal font and dedicated him in Christian baptism to Christ and the church. We believe that Christ died for infants and all other innocent ones, that such belong to God's people by Christian claim, and that they are saved if they die in innocence — not *because* they've been baptized nor just *because* they're innocent but because of Christ's universal atonement. In this faith we baptized them and in this faith we instructed them. We expected them to enter personally into a meaningful knowledge of Christ when the Holy Spirit made them aware of need.

Although it was their free choice, in this also our sons met our expectations. Each, in his own time and according to his own development, came to the place of personal commitment to Christ. We brought them into church membership as juniors after careful instruction. They came to adult commitment and full assurance of faith later in high school and college days.

Our youngest son Charles offers a most dramatic illustration of how God calls His own and makes Himself known in personal revelation. I have in my files a "red letter" written by him when he was in his third year in college. (He actually used red ink!)

Prior to that time, Chuck had seemed to conform easily to the pattern of a Christian home.

"I can't understand why anyone who's been raised as a Christian wouldn't be one," he said one day to his mother.

They had been speaking of a family in the church whose children were rejecting Christ's way.

We knew, however, throughout his high school and early college days, that Chuck's faith continued to be formal and nominal. He had accepted Christ as a child would. He evidenced little of the struggle of the soul and even less of the triumphant victory of one who has met God, who has seen himself in the presence of the Holy One and experienced cleansing.

Deloris and I prayed earnestly for Chuck as we had for his older brothers. We could settle for nothing less than full commitment for each of our boys. We had seen too many cool, half-hearted, partially-committed, nominal Christians in the churches we had served.

Three weeks before we received Chuck's letter, we had visited him at school. We sensed at that time that he was in the midst of spiritual conflict. The vitality of the Christian witness surrounding him on a Christian campus was getting to him. We came away only to redouble our efforts in prayer.

As I quote from his letter today I can feel the exultation of that day when word came of answered prayers.

"Last night was a new and thrilling experience for me," he wrote on December 6, 1963. "For the first time in my life I really entered into an experience with God. My attitude this whole semester has been very bad. . .I never told anyone, but I decided some time ago that I wasn't a Christian and probably never really had been. I had prayed several times this semester to try to reach God, but it always seemed like I was talking to myself. I began to wonder if there was a God at all."

He had had some angry words with his girlfriend that evening, it seems, and he went to his room to find a place alone for thought and prayer.

"I started to pray and it was the same old story of nothing, but I soon decided that I wasn't going to stop until I found God."

He waited there in prayer longer than he thought, for he wrote: "Shortly I just knew it had happened. I can't explain it, but it was what I had heard people testify of and I wondered if they really knew what they were talking about. Just all of a sudden my burden lifted. My first reaction was one of disbelief. It was sort of like Kennedy getting shot — I knew it had happened but I couldn't believe it! I looked at my watch and I had been praying almost an hour and a half. I found that hard to believe too because I suppose the longest I had prayed before was about ten minutes!"

He concluded his letter with a word that should challenge every Christian parent. "Well, there is not much to say. I had often wondered if you and other Christians really had an experience with God or if you were just talking. Well, now I know."

Deloris and I appreciate the assistance of the church in bringing our sons into living faith in Christ. In the life of each son there were significant persons outside the family who were our helpers.

Hartwell and Ann Smith were two of these. They were Sunday school teachers (team teaching) for our high school class in Toronto when John and Stan were of that age. Sharp young adults, professionally trained and utterly committed to Christ, they were beautiful people. Just what our youth needed to challenge them. Our boys were profoundly influenced.

Stanley Walters was a young professor in the department of religion at Greenville College when Chuck entered as a freshman. All students there are required to take two courses in Bible. Chuck continued to opt for a Bible course each semester until he had been in all of Professor Walters' classes.

Who can say where credit should be given? Many others who cannot be named witnessed to our sons by life and word. The boys saw in the church those examples of wholeness and beauty which are to be found wherever Christians gather for fellowship and worship. They found, as I did in my own youth, in the family and the church, a source of the spiritual reality all need for abundant living.

It seemed natural for them to take a positive attitude toward the church. They didn't find perfection in either the home or the church, I'm sure, but they didn't seem to flip because of that. John pointedly reproved a friend one day for bitterly criticizing the church: "Come on, Harry! I've never known the church to be like you describe it. We're old enough now, aren't we, to know what a rich heritage we have because of the church?"

Deloris and I have lived long enough to know. We know we've had help from the church in the most important responsibility God ever gave us — the rearing of three sons. Numerous "godfathers" and "godmothers," undesignated but willing volunteers, have served with us to bring our boys to a knowledge of God. We heartily appreciate them all.

We recall blunders and sad mistakes. I take some comfort in the knowledge that we're no different from all parents in this. Our sons are now in a position as fathers to understand the failures of their own father. But one blunder troubles me yet after all the years. I gave one of our sons a spanking after he was fourteen years old! I can scarcely believe it today!

His infraction of the rules of the home was serious enough to warrant discipline. He came in at two o'clock Sunday morning when he knew that he had to be home by eleven o'clock that Saturday night. I had let him attend a ball game at the Canadian National Exhibition with some friends of his own age although my permission had been granted with some misgivings. I was not pleased with the boys he was going with. Instead of coming directly home after the game he was persuaded to loiter along the midway with the others.

I came home late that evening myself. I had worked in my office at the church until almost midnight and when I came in I found my wife very worried, so we both waited up.

It was a sad scene. For half an hour I talked with him, trying to impress him with our concern for his moral well-being as well as for his physical safety. I wish I had stopped with that. But I ended the session by spanking him in front of his mother, as though he were a child. He was humiliated. I am still ashamed.

There must be better ways to discipline than to humiliate a son or daughter. The force of my blows was not enough to leave any marks on him. But there are other kinds of bruises. Sometimes these psychological hurts remain long afterwards to trouble relationships.

I accept my blame for the crisis on this occasion. I should not have given permission for him to go with friends I didn't trust. How much better if I had made time to take him and his brothers to the exhibition. We could have made it a family affair. And when things did go wrong and discipline was necessary, I overreacted. The young man was not that difficult to reason with.

You can be sure I've apologized to my son and we've talked of this since he became a father. He assures me of forgiveness and understanding. Our relationship is open and warm. But I goofed. And, though this may have been one of the bad times, it certainly wasn't the only mistake I've made in bringing up three sons. I wonder now why a strapping fourteen-year-old let me get by with such punishment! I didn't think then of the possibility that he might rebel but what could I have done had he refused to let me spank him? I know now that his submission indicated how much he respected the authority of his father and how deeply he felt his own wrong-doing at the moment. He was an obedient son at heart, but I allowed my fears to betray my best judgment.

However, it is my experience that discipline is necessary. Responsibility demands accountability. A parent can't escape the duty to discipline and train a child if he takes seriously his responsibility. Concerned love was being demonstrated when we corrected our children. It showed we cared. But discipline should express love rather than fear.

I'm confident our sons knew we loved them even when we enforced discipline. My life has been a busy one, but I have spent time with our sons. We often had to schedule the hours of family "togetherness" but there was no burden of duty in it. We love to play games and Deloris and I still play together, but usually Scrabble these days. Our sons and I have had many times together competing at ping pong, bowling, or Rook. We've made up a foursome for golf again and again. I've known one of us to cancel out of another foursome in order to play together.

The touring trips we've been able to make as a family have been important. There were many, but three of them I'll never forget. One, in the summer of 1947, took us in a complete circle of Lake Michigan. Another several years later, from Toronto to Washington, D.C. All three of our sons were with us for these. On the third trip only the youngest was still at home, and he was scarcely there very often. He had just graduated from college, in 1965, and was to be married two months later.

I had responsibilities in the state of Washington that June, and Deloris and I took Chuck with us. We motored to Seattle, then along the coast southward to Los Angeles, and home again. Having just left dormitory food, Chuck began the first night out by ordering steak for dinner. The next night he ordered shrimp. Then the third day steak again! I cried out for help then, asking him to remember economy! We enjoyed all three weeks of wonderful fellowship — weeks that bring a sense of nostalgia as I write.

I like to think that Chuck spoke for all of our sons when he said to my congregation in Indianapolis: "You know our dad as your pastor. But we know him as a friend." The occasion was a surprise program, "This Is Your Life, Pastor Ellis." Many fine things were said that day. Many of them have faded in memory. But I can't forget that a son called me a friend!

We expected our sons to grow up. They were never tied to the apron strings of their mother nor did they depend upon their father to make all their decisions, or to find employment for them.

Deliberately and with purpose we gave increasing responsibility to each of them, graded to their development. One promise we held before the boys was that each could learn to drive and be trusted with the car when he was old enough to be licensed. It was before the days of driving instruction in every school, so I became their instructor. They learned well. They drove without accident. And they've never let me forget that during those early days of their driving I spoiled our family record by backing the car into a tree when we were at the lake!

We expected them to make choices for themselves as they developed. Stan was fifteen when he asked if he could attend the movie, "The Jackie Robinson Story." We had never taken them to movies nor permitted them to attend as children. You can imagine his surprise when I promptly gave my permission. He was drying dishes for his mother. I left the room and Stan asked with unbelief, "Mom, did Dad really mean it? Did he say I can go?"

His mother replied: "Yes, Stan, you heard him."

"Do you think he wants me to go?" he asked.

"I don't know, Stan," Deloris replied. "But I do know he wants you to learn to make your own decisions about what is right and wrong. We can't always be with you to decide for you."

Stan didn't go. Not then. He just couldn't believe I was willing, though I had given my permission. He held his parents in too high regard to willingly displease them. I would have been quite happy for him to have gone. It was a good film. But beyond that, I know that a person never becomes an adult until he or she knows how to discern the difference between the will of the parent and the will of God. The parents' will and God's will may often agree. Whether or not they do, the young adult must be able to identify the will of God for himself.

The acceptance of increasing responsibility meant for our sons a large measure of self-support beginning in high school and continuing through college. They learned early that no task is too menial if it is honest and serves a good purpose. They delighted us with their ambition and initiative.

Sometimes they frightened us too. Once John asked us if he could use his bicycle and get a job delivering fish and chips. We lived in Toronto. He was fifteen. Streets were narrow in our section of the city and traffic was terrific. We had witnessed an accident involving a young boy making deliveries on a bicycle just a short time before. Deloris would not hear of John's running the risk.

Then one day he came in with joyful news. He had secured a job at the hardware store two blocks from us. Mother was relieved until some weeks later when we learned about his job. He was delivering sacks, bags of feed, garden tools and ladders on a bicycle furnished by the owner of the store!

Throughout our sons' schooling we've supported them with our encouragement, our prayers, and whatever was absolutely necessary in finances. They have appreciated our assistance, I'm sure. They know, however, and we are pleased, that they have earned their way and learned how to bear responsibility for money.

Our greatest joy in this regard comes when we see the faithful stewardship of these adult sons. Early on, when they began to have an allowance, we taught them to tithe. As a family, we believe that all we are and have are God's gifts to us. We must give back to God the whole of life, including talents, time and wealth. Stewardship of life requires proportionate giving, therefore, that others may be reached with the gospel and share in the blessings of the abundant life.

Pastor James Persons, of Lincroft, New Jersey, wrote recently in an unsolicited letter: "Your son and his family continue to be a source of great blessing and support in my efforts here in the gospel. They are an example and encouragement to many." He referred to our eldest son, John. I believe the pastor of Stan and Chuck in Indianapolis would say the same of them and their families.

When I was in university God gave me a promise from 1 Samuel 2:30: "Those that honor me I will honor." In that moment of great surrender, I promised that I would do my best to honor God and depend upon His promise.

God has fulfilled that promise in our family. He has fulfilled that promise in the stalwart Christian character of our sons. Other honors have come, I suppose some would tell me, but I could not ask for a greater honor from God than the joy of fathering three such sons. My best wish to each of them is that their children may bring to them the joy they have brought to their mother and me.

One should correct a child not by hurting him but by persuading him.

Menander—an ancient author

VERLYN AND LOUISE BEARDSLEE, *Edna and Hugh White, and Ruth Evelyn and Glenn White, on the occasion of the White's 50th anniversary in 1975.*

Hugh A. White

Hugh A. White, *a spry septuagenarian, has proven himself a rare talent in the realm of finance. Across a long and active lifetime he could have directed this skill to personal ends; instead, early in his career he saw vast possibilities in the Christian management of possessions for God, and he began to use money as a medium for Christian ministry.*

As a certified public accountant and trustee of charitable foundations, Hugh has counselled several millions of dollars into charities both Christian and secular. As well, when he and his wife Edna have been confronted by needs in North America and other parts of the world, they have responded generously. Those who know him best know his high quality of stewardship.

His son Glenn, a vice president of Chrysler Corporation, is a member of the board of directors of the Boy Scouts of America and the Children's Hospital in Detroit. In 1976 Glenn served as vice chairman of the Billy Graham Crusade held in the Silver Dome, Pontiac, Michigan.

Glenn and his father both sit on the board of trustees of Spring Arbor College, a Christian liberal arts school located west of Jackson, Michigan where the Hugh A. White library is.

Louise W. Beardslee, daughter of the Hugh Whites and mother of four children, lives with her husband Verlyn and family in Dearborn, Michigan. In her professional life she was an elementary school principal. She now carries on a family tradition by taking an active part in the Sunday School of the Dearborn Free Methodist Church where they are members.

Hugh White and his wife live in Bloomfield Hills northwest of Detroit.

Telling about my family and the kind of father I was in that family may sound like bragging. However, I like to think of this story as a thankful recounting of a fulfilling relationship. I remember Bishop Charles Fairbairn saying at an annual conference once: "There are two kinds of pride — Texas pride and Michigan pride. Michigan pride is not sinful." I am from Michigan. I am proud of my family.

As a businessman, a certified public accountant, I enjoy preparing financial statements, analyzing investments and working on tax law problems. I would rather write about these subjects than about my role as a Christian father. But I have been blessed along with my wife Edna to have raised two children, Glenn and Louise, who have gone on with their spouses to raise their children — seven in all — in much the same style as we. Jesus Christ and His Church are the fabric of their lives. And now I have two great-grandchildren who are getting much the same "treatment" from their parents.

Since God has done so much for me, I'm glad to write about what He has taught me. If recounting my family's development is helpful to other families or young couples preparing for marriage, then this writing will have been worthwhile.

Our family is extremely close. This closeness, which we have kept over many years, is linked to a certain continuity in our lives — a continuity noticeably absent in our fast-paced times. For example, I have lived most of my life in Michigan. Both my wife and I were born and raised in this state. We raised our families here and are seeing our grandchildren raised in Birmingham and Dearborn, close to our home in Bloomfield Hills. These three cities are suburbs of Detroit.

Forming another strand of continuity in our lives is the fact that we have always attended and worked in churches in the Free Methodist denomination. My wife was raised a Methodist and my family goes back two generations in the Free Methodist Church.

Glenn and his wife Ruth Evelyn live close enough to attend the Ferndale church with us. Two of their children and spouses also attend there. We sit together and fill one pew.

My daughter Louise, her husband Verlyn, and their four children live about twenty miles away and attend the Dearborn church. Sometimes they also attend church with us, and we flow into two pews.

Worshiping together is the cornerstone on which the several generations of our family are built. We've found that when children and grandchildren share the same love of God, then common beliefs, interests and goals grow in the family. These in turn foster family unity.

As you would expect, I want to tell you in more depth about the key parts worship, honesty and discipline have played in our home. But I have to explain that these emphases came to us fairly naturally. We didn't read manuals on how to raise children. We drew primarily on common sense, the experiences of our own families, and the teachings of the Bible. But there was one simple feature in our family that bound us together through all our experiences. We simply enjoyed being together and having fun together. The matters of honesty, discipline and other principles were natural parts of being a Christian family with the support of tradition and training, and they took work. The everyday fact of our family, however, was simply an immense enjoyment of each other.

We played games together — table games, golf, baseball, and we swam together too. We had devotions together, went to church together, sat and talked with each other, told stories and laughed. When the kids were still small we started playing tennis together. I remember my wife once whispered to me during a game, "Just let them win every once in a while." I replied, "No, let them win when they can — they're not going to win just because I gave it to them." I don't remember any problems with competitiveness either.

I must admit that I was away from the family too much as the children were growing up. As a partner in a growing Detroit accounting firm, with offices also in Chicago and New York, and as a tax accountant and witness in many court trials throughout the United States, I was extremely busy. I telephoned the family during the week and wrote letters when I was away on business. Often my wife and children were able to join me on the weekends when I was in a city not too far away. But when we were all together at home, the fact of our love and enjoyment of each other seemed to build up a reservoir of love for the times I had to be away.

I also have to admit that even when I was working in the Detroit area, our dinners often had to be late and I could not be directly involved in the children's play and school activities as much as I wished. One way of making up for this was to have them travel with me occasionally on business trips. One extensive court case took me to Louisville, Kentucky. When I learned how long the job was going to take, I had the family come join me. We were there fourteen months. Glenn started kindergarten there at age five. Louise was three then.

When I was in Cincinnati on one phase of the case during our Kentucky stay, the family would come up and spend weekends with me. I was only a little more than one hundred miles from them. One time they came up expecting that I would be finished with that phase of my work and would return to Louisville with them. I couldn't get away until the next week so they stayed over the weekend with me. My wife hadn't brought extra clothes or pajamas for the children, so they wore my shirts for pajamas. The sleeves were, of course, too long, and I can still see those two gleeful little kids jumping from one bed to another in our hotel room saying, "We're birds! We're birds!"

Through experiences like this, traveling has become part of the character of our family. We all love to travel. When the children were young my wife literally had to keep a suitcase packed and ready at all times. She used to say to people, "I have to be ready or we might be left behind!"

I worked hard and was busy, yes, but our life certainly was not all work and no play. Once I was asked at a convention on investments, "What is the best investment you ever made?" Without hesitating, I answered, "The money and time I have spent on vacations with my family."

Vacations together were one way we were able to be together for high quality times. They have evolved from tenting to renting accommodations, but the family closeness has remained constant. When the children were small, we all took our two weeks' vacation together. We loaded the car with swim suits, golf bags and tennis rackets. Several of these vacations come flooding over my memory as I mention them.

In 1936 we drove to New York City, arriving in time to attend a Good Friday service at a church on Wall Street. Then we sailed to Bermuda for a week's visit. Once there, we lived on the ship, rode bikes (Mother and Dad on a tandem, the kids on singles), swam, hiked, played golf and attended Easter services in a great field of lilies. We heard Homer Rodeheaver speak, and his sister Ruth Thomas sing. We struck up a friendship with her and her husband there that continues to this day.

Another time, when Glenn and Louise were about fifteen and twelve, we drove across Canada to Banff National Park in Alberta, and then on south to San Francisco and Los Angeles. We sold our car there in California and came back to Michigan by train. One of the things we did to interest the kids while traveling was play car games. My wife was a teacher so she always liked to have them learning something. We would see who could name the states and their capitals, the justices of the Supreme Court and our congressmen and senators. We also played games that taught Scripture. The object of one game, which aided in Scripture memorization, was to work through the alphabet, quoting verses that started with the different letters. Once, when we were traveling through the western states, we got all the way to "X" and it was my turn to quote. Without hesitating, I said, "Xerxes the king said, 'Let us alone.' " Glenn said, "Dad, where's that? I never saw that in my Bible." So I had to admit I made it up.

These vacations continued on through college and to our joy, continue virtually every summer yet. It is not uncommon for Glenn to phone up in the spring and say: "Here are the weeks I can get free this summer. Mark them down." Then we all plan where to go. I have always tried to arrange my vacations so we could be together.

In 1946 Glenn graduated from the University of Michigan and Lou from high school. They voted we spend five weeks traveling through the west by car, as graduation presents. We took a "reconnaissance" side trip to Grand Rapids to play golf with Dr. Clarence Snyder, and for Glenn to see Dr. Snyder's daughter Ruth Evelyn whom he eventually was to marry. Her parents did not know of this courtship at the time, however, and things got a little complicated, but it all worked out.

We stuck together as a family on these trips. Glenn and I played forty-five holes of golf in one session at Colorado Springs. The last four holes my nose was bleeding from too much exercise at high levels. I suggested we stop but he wanted to finish the eighteen because he had just evened the score.

Even though by that time I had blood on my face and on the front of my shirt, I agreed. Then we asked permission to play through two foursomes. The people in charge took one look at my face and shirt, probably thought we were crazy, and said, "By all means, go on." When we arrived back at the hotel, Edna exclaimed, "Daddy, what happened?" Glenn said, "He tried to cheat and I hit him with my putter."

Glenn has become a very good golfer and I keep insisting that he play with better players, but he still arranges for me to play in his foursomes, which I appreciate.

Since our children have married, we have vacationed together in Northern Michigan, North Carolina, Arizona and Alberta, among other spots. One summer, we went to Europe for three weeks with Glenn and Ruth Evelyn and their children. A few years later, we did the same with Lou, Verlyn and their four children.

Our family, like all families, was not all a matter of fun and games. There was the whole business of growing up, with lessons to be learned and discipline problems to be dealt with. Our primary concern was that our children respect us and the church. We found it helpful to have lots of church people in our home. The kids got to know and respect them and what the church was doing. They were always interested because we included them in everything, from the time they could talk.

We had many ministers and missionaries in our home, and we did a lot of entertaining for special guests who had come to our church, such as quartets and other singing groups, so we named our guest room the "Prophet's Chamber." That practice meant a lot to our family and tied our children in a good way to the church.

My wife has been called "Mrs. Sunday School," for the

more than forty years she was Sunday School teacher, superintendent of the primary department and general superintendent. We were both involved in our local church, the conference and the general church. We feel this gave our children a sense of Christian priorities for themselves and their families. Once my wife asked me to go down and straighten out a grade three class. She said, "Just come down for a couple of weeks." There were two boys who were kind of obstreperous. I went to calm them down and ended up staying with a children's class for twenty-two years. This kind of commitment could not fail to give our children a feeling for the church as an important place, requiring commitment. In fact, some of our grandchildren and their spouses are teachers and superintendents of classes and departments in their churches.

I have been on the Board of Administration of our denomination since 1947, as well as on the Commission on Missions and many other committees. One never knows exactly what will influence his children, but I feel sure this involvement affected my children for the good. Lou and Verlyn live within walking distance of their church in Dearborn — closeness to church was one of their requirements when buying a house. They are involved now in a relocation project their church is going through. I've had Glenn on several committees I have chaired at our local church and at Spring Arbor College, Michigan, where I have served as chairman of the board since the mid-fifties. He and I don't agree on every little thing, but he has been a tremendous help to me. He is a great organizer. As he puts it, our lives have become deeply intertwined because we play together and we work together.

Edna and I were so busy with church matters that someone from our congregation once said our children by rights should have turned out to be juvenile delinquents! But we didn't neglect them in it all.

Entertaining church people at home did have its effect on the children. We took a pretty rigorous stand about going to movies, and drinking and dancing. But our children never had serious trouble with family regulations, partly, I think, because they had more influences on them than just their parents. The people they admired had much the same approach to these things as we, and were a great support to us.

The Prophet's Chamber and church involvement also had a key part to play in the conversions of our two children. Glenn was converted while in high school at an evangelistic service in our church. Lou also gave her life to Christ in our church. Both were in their teens. These commitments and what led up to them have made all the difference in their lives and the life of our whole family.

It pleased us that both our children stayed in the Free Methodist Church, but my wife and I always said that loving the Lord and serving Him were most important, whatever church they might choose. We give God the praise that our children and families are strongly Christian. We know other couples who prayed and worked just as hard with their families only to have their children rebel. We were very fortunate.

I've said we took an active part in the decisions of our children. That even extended to romance, although they may not even realize this now. Glenn went with girls near us in Birmingham. I remember his mother didn't like one of them at all and didn't think she was the right sort of girl for him and she very kindly but firmly let him know it. She was the same with Lou — not meddlesome, just concerned and frank. She subtly steered her away from a few young men.

I also had something to do with their romances. As I said earlier, Glenn's wife Ruth Evelyn is the daughter of close family friends. When Glenn went to the University of Michigan, Ruth Evelyn was there attending graduate school. She roomed with Grace, Bishop Mark Ormston's daughter. Our former pastor's son Wes Stephenson was there also.

One day I said to Glenn, "You know, what you and Wes ought to do is make a practice once a week of taking Grace and Ruth Evelyn out to dinner for Christian fellowship." They did, and while the fellowship remained Christian, it became something else as well! The outcome: Glenn and Ruth Evelyn White, and Dr. Wesley and Grace Stephenson.

Lou and Verlyn had attended Spring Arbor College together, here in Michigan, and they kept company while they were there. For a variety of reasons, that romance broke up — but temporarily. Verlyn was a close friend of the Dale

Crydermans, also family friends of ours. The Crydermans spoke well of him. I started writing to Verlyn who was on duty in Japan, primarily to keep in touch with young men from our church who were serving overseas. Then Lou started writing to him again. It had become clear after I had received a few letters from him that he was really writing to Lou. So they got back together and I'd have to say I had some influence on that courtship too.

My wife says I was firm but not strict with the children. As they grew up, they knew they had to be responsible for their actions. We tried to help them understand that they had responsibilities. For instance, if they took a book out of the library and didn't take it back in time, it was clearly their responsibility to return it and pay the fine. We weren't going to do it for them.

Lou, being a girl, didn't require much "physical assistance" in discipline. Stern words were enough for her. But Glenn remembers several occasions when he was told, after some misdemeanor, that when Daddy got home he would "deal with him." Sure enough, when I got home, already alerted to the crime, he and I would go downstairs to the makeshift woodshed — a pile of logs and odds and ends of wood behind the furnace — and I would tell him to pick the switch. He didn't always pick the strongest switch. A few times it broke and we ended up laughing. I never could finish those particular "correcting efforts," but in general I did not spare the rod, nor did I spoil the child.

One reason we moved from Detroit to the suburbs was that we felt the school system would be better. There also turned out to be more social activities for the children. This made it more difficult for us in a way, because we wanted to have the primary influence within our home while the children were young, so they could learn to stand on their own two feet when they were older.

But openness overcame that problem, as it proved to do all through the growing up years. They were open with us about all their activities and various courtships. When Glenn was in high school, he would come home at night, whistling as he came up the front walk and then up the stairs. We were in bed, and I could tell he was stopping at the top of the stairs. His mother would just have to say,

"Glenn," and he would bounce into the room and tell us about what went on that evening. After a while I would say, "Goodnight, goodnight," but they always liked to talk things out.

And Lou remains extremely close to her mother. Edna belongs to a literary club and she always invites Lou to come over to that once a month, and then they have lunch together. They like to have me join them if I can get free for lunch, but they also enjoy just being together.

If it is true that I have avoided being too strict with my kids, my own father must have had something to do with it. He was a farmer and ran a co-op store. I was not as close to my father as my children are to me. Of course, we lived a different type of life on the farm. I always had great respect for my father. He was very active in the church — a Sunday School teacher and a delegate to conference. In fact, he represented the North Michigan Conference and I the Southern Michigan at three general conferences we attended together.

I never really played with my father the way Glenn and Lou and I played together, but my father was smart about a lot of things. I remember in particular an incident with a new race horse we had that wasn't broken yet. I wanted to break it, so the hired man, my brother and I hooked it up to a good buggy. It was a crazy thing to do. We started driving it. But we had hitched up the horse with a light harness and when the horse reared up, it broke the reins and ran away, badly damaging the buggy.

Dad was in the living room watching all these antics. I was scared he would jump all over us. But he didn't holler at us at all. He said we'd have to learn that when you're trying to break a colt, you have to have reins that are strong enough to control it. He was a teacher to us. He could have been severe, even to calling us stupid dumbbells.

I think my father instilled a certain honesty in me and I have seen this in my children. He was a member of the Township Board. A meeting was called by the chairman and as the meeting started, Dad saw there was no real business to care for. It became clear the meeting had been called to allow the board members to collect attendance fees. My father refused to take the fee. God blessed him for his decision and his business associates and neighbors respected him.

I've tried to pass this honesty down to my children. It hasn't hurt either of them in business or family life. It has never meant demotion or loss of jobs when they have had to stand up for their convictions. The long term benefits, both spiritual and material, have been proved over and over.

A lasting story from the accounting firm where I started out comes to mind. It is a story I was fond of telling my children. I'm sure telling it was partly my way of giving them a model for their own hard times that would come.

I was working on a very important, secret job with my boss and another young accountant. We had nearly completed the job and the boss had chosen me to accompany him to New York for a conference with the officers for whom the work was being done. I was excited — it was a big thing to go to New York.

As we drew up the final report and prepared schedules to accompany it, my boss instructed me to prepare a schedule in a certain manner to illustrate what he wanted to prove. But the facts would not support that conclusion. I told him I would not do it that way as it would be misleading and deceptive. He insisted. When I refused again, he grabbed the telephone and called the office manager and said, "White's defying me, I want you to come over here right away." I put my feet up on the window sill and just sat there. Two things ran through my mind — that I had probably lost my job, or at least my chance to go to New York. I was young and, I guess, a little stubborn.

We prepared the schedule to set forth the facts accurately. My boss neither looked at me nor spoke to me for the balance of the afternoon. Much to my surprise, at dinner that night, he said, "White, why not take your wife with you to New York?" I said I'd like to but couldn't afford it. He said the company would pay. Then he turned to the office manager from the Washington office, who was working with us, and told him to find accommodations for us in Washington, show us the town and help us get on to New York. I believe he appreciated the fact that I had stuck to my principles.

While honesty and responsibility were emphasized in our family, it was all a part of the atmosphere of enjoying each other. That's what carried us through any rough times. Glenn and Lou have said while this chapter was being prepared that we always made them feel important in whatever they were doing — important to the whole direction our family was taking. This made them conscientious about doing the right thing. They did not want to reflect poorly on the nature of our family.

When we were first married we were very poor but have prospered over the years. The Lord has blessed us. Stewardship was always important to us. We believed "things" are a trust from God for us to manage. We went through the depression years and barely made ends meet, but even then we felt stewardship was not only scriptural but crucial to the well-being of our family.

Following graduation from the University of Michigan in 1928, I went to work for a public accounting firm in Detroit at $140 a month. Lou was born the following February. We were buying a car and household furniture and furnishings, and were trying to pay off a school debt on top of that. Then the bank where we had our checking account closed down. We didn't have much money on deposit there but the loss was a blow nonetheless. God knew about it and cared. Within a few weeks my boss called me into his office and gave me a $500 advance which he soon turned into a bonus. What a lift!

We made a practice of holding family discussions on our charitable contributions. I remember well one of these discussions when the children were eight and eleven. We sat down together and determined that over and above our regular giving we should give several hundred dollars. We suggested to the children that they come up with a plan for the distribution of the extra amount. A few evenings later they came back with a plan to use the funds to help the lower paid pastors of our conference. They had taken the conference minutes and had worked out the schedule for the disbursement. We approved the plan and the whole family received great joy in carrying it out.

Thinking back on the providences that have led to the continued closeness of our family, my advice to Christian fathers raising young families is simple and basic:

• Put Christ first in everything you do. Let your children know how important He is. Have devotions together, attend church regularly, and sit together. Be a significant part of the life of your church for your church's sake, your sake and your children's sake.

• Take pride in your family name. A realistic family pride keeps children striving to bring honor to the family in their actions. It restrains them in the temptations children face as they grow up. As the head of the home, you must live up to your own ideals in the presence of your wife and children.

• Involve your children, in keeping with their age and abilities, in planning stewardship, church involvement, family outings and vacations. This shows them how important they are in the family.

• Be united with your wife on disciplinary matters. Don't allow your children to play one parent off against the other. Every child tries this and if it becomes ingrained it can cause havoc.

• Don't give your children a choice about doing something only to try to change their minds if they choose irresponsibly. If you give them the choice, you must then let the child go through with it. And be judicious about what choices you give them.

As I look back on our family life, I realize that this story should be about Mrs. White — not me. She was a genius with the kids — a marvellous mother to them. When I remember the little touches that mean so much to a family's growth, Edna is always in the picture. She never let me go to work without first eating a good breakfast with me. She never came to the dining room table with curlers in her hair or wearing a housecoat. When I would come home after long days or even weeks of work, she always looked so nice and had the children dressed for dinner and waiting anxiously for their Daddy.

Those little touches, repeated hundreds, perhaps thousands of times, accumulate to make a family what it is. And my wife orchestrated all those details.

When a father, who is now seventy-seven, looks back over such a rich, rewarding life, he remembers the small incidents again. Such as Glenn's accompanying me on a business trip to Milwaukee when he was eight. He stayed in a hotel with me and bought presents for his mother and sister, just like a little businessman. Or the birthday telegram we sent to Louise in her schoolroom — and we weren't even out of town! Or the traditional ice cream outings after the kids had performed in band and choir concerts at school.

In fact, as I finish putting down these memories, one of the strongest that comes back is of getting off the train, coming down the street and seeing Glenn and Louise, freshly cleaned and dressed, waiting on the porch for me. As soon as I came into view, they left the porch and ran to me.

It's great to remember being welcomed home after a long day's work.

A father who is always threatening does not receive much reverence.

Menander—an ancient author

JOY IS SHARED as two proud parents exchange flowers before father walks their daughter down the aisle. Kathleen, Carolyn, and Donald Bastian.

Donald N. Bastian

As I introduce myself, I must tell you first that I was a pastor for twenty-one years in Kentucky, British Columbia, and Illinois. During those years I carried on an extensive counseling ministry and saw how shaky domestic life in North America is — even within the church. Then and since, I have tried to use biblical resources to strengthen and enrich family life.

During my past five years as a bishop of the Free Methodist Church of North America I have tried to maintain a special place in my speaking schedule for the nurture of family life.

Kathleen and I have four children.

Carolyn, our first, has added a certain quality of feminine grace to our home. A school teacher, she and her husband Douglas, a director with Admiral of Canada, live in Toronto where both are active in Kingsview Free Methodist Church.

Donald Gregory, our second child, is an editor and writer who with his wife June Yamamoto Bastian also lives in the western end of Metro Toronto. Don's special training for writing is a master's degree in philosophy from St. Louis University.

Robert is a medical doctor who resides in St. Louis, Missouri, where he is doing a residency in head and neck surgery. His loyalty has long been drawn between medicine and music, a conflict not yet resolved, and he hopes to keep a large place for both in his life.

Our youngest child John David is our retarded son. Since he was three years old he has spent his time in Woodlands School in British Columbia.

It was evening and life was winding down in our brown-stuccoed parsonage. The older three children had gone to their rooms and were in the final stages of preparing for bed. Carolyn was eleven; Donald, eight; Robert, six, and John David was our baby.

I went upstairs to the boys' room and sat down on the brown hooked rug between their two single beds. I did this often when I was home and the children welcomed it.

Both boys were on their beds but not yet under the covers. I asked how things had gone that October day and got their eager reports: a tiff on the playground and a special word of praise from a teacher. Robert was in grade one and Donald in grade three.

I had already learned that bedtime was one of the best times of the day for a father to talk to his children. They were not eager to go to sleep, so talk flowed easily. Moreover, with the world shut out and darkness settling, distractions were at a minimum.

But perhaps most important, when the children began to relax before sleep came, their real hurts and joys — matters submerged by the demands of the day — began to bubble to the surface.

After we had chatted a few minutes, I said to the boys: "Let me have a prayer with you before you go to sleep." They welcomed this too, partly at least, because lights out would be further delayed. I prayed with them and went downstairs.

I stopped in the kitchen of our New Westminster, British Columbia, parsonage, but I can't remember why. My wife Kathleen was in the other bedroom upstairs with Carolyn and John David. Suddenly I heard footsteps on the stairs, and in a moment around the corner came Donald. Something was on his mind.

"Remember the missionary offering you took two Sundays ago?" he asked. I remembered.

"And remember how much I've wanted a two-wheel bike?" I remembered that also.

"Well," he continued, "after that Sunday I went up to some houses and asked people for money for the missionaries. But I knew I was going to keep it for my bike."

"Did you get anything?" I asked.

"Mrs. Bird gave me a quarter."

We were talking very quietly and seriously. I was face to face with a nine-year-old with a conscience problem.

"Do you want me to go with you to see Mrs. Bird and take the quarter back?"

He could do it by himself he assured me, and I was willing to let him try. He disappeared around the corner, mounting the stairs to his room more buoyantly than he had come down them.

Only moments later came the sound of bare feet on the stairs again. I was still in the kitchen and I wondered if he had more to say. But this time it was our six-year-old Robert who rounded the corner. Though younger, he was taller than Donald.

He too had something he wanted to tell me and he got to the point very quickly. At the back of his grade one room under the windows there was a cupboard in which his teacher had placed some packets of unlined paper for classroom use. They had apparently caught his eye. Across several days he had collected eight or ten packets, stashed them in his desk, and then brought them all home. He still had them.

I had found it difficult enough to know whether I should let a grade three child make amends on his own but at that moment I felt a lad in grade one was not up to it.

"Do you want me to go with you to tell your teacher and take the paper back?" I asked.

The answer should have been yes, but not from Robert. He has always loved the challenge of doing things on his own. As a small child he wanted to cross streets on his own. Later, he bought his own ten-speed bike. On his own initiative, he took his last year of high school by correspondence (with money earned from janitorial work) thereby telescoping two years into one. He even found a challenge in administering his own haircuts.

"No," he said to my question, "I can do it."

I gave both boys a couple of days, then I phoned Mrs. Bird. Yes, Donald had returned the quarter with apologies. I phoned the teacher. Yes, Robert had come to her, returning the paper and saying he was sorry.

Looking back, it seems that night was a crucial episode in the life of my sons, but it happened because I had taken time to be with them and in these special moments to ask how things were going.

I've heard that children need quality time with their parents, and especially their fathers, and I believe it. I recall taking a few minutes to play hopscotch with my daughter or to hold a conversation with her and her doll. I remember romping on the floor with a three-year-old son and taking a bike ride on country roads with a boy in his early teens.

These episodes out of our life together took place in widely separated places. Our pilgrimage as a family began in a one room apartment just west of Toronto. We moved from there southwest to Greenville, Illinois, where I finished college and then to Lexington, Kentucky, where I finished seminary. New Westminster, British Columbia, a half continent away, beckoned us when a Free Methodist Church there needed a young pastor to give them pastoral leadership. Five years later we returned to Greenville, Illinois, where I was college church pastor for thirteen years. We now live back in Toronto.

Carolyn, now married and soon to present us with a grandchild, reminds me yet of the time when I took her out to a little restaurant on the edge of Greenville for lunch. Her mother was cooking for a group at church and the boys were at school. Carolyn was a freshman in college. What impressed her at the time, she tells me, was her father's willingness to spend the time with her alone. She apparently perceived this as quality time.

Once back in New Westminster when she was only eight I was trying to help a young man win a battle against the bottle. He was a keen fellow, sharp of mind and genteel — a pleasure to be with. I took him for a walk in a Vancouver park and asked Carolyn to go along. He and I chatted and she amused herself, skipping up to me every now and then with a question. Often, to my friend's amusement, she would be off again before the question was answered. She apparently just wanted to touch base with her father.

I remember much earlier sitting by that same little girl in church when she was four and I was still a college student in southern Illinois. She was a joy to touch and I recall the rustle of her crisp nylon organdy dress. I also remember the quiet spring twilight when she and I walked home from church, her hand in mine, and she saw the pale new moon in the sky. It looks like your finger nail, she said. She didn't yet know the word cuticle. Perhaps she was three. These were all quality moments, even though I didn't know it at the time.

Yet my record isn't unblemished. More than once the press of modern life worked subtly against my wife and me, to the children's detriment. By the time we had been in the brown-stuccoed New Westminster parsonage a year, the church next door was humming. The church was a new L-shaped facility, just completed by the heroic labors of the membership. Because it was larger than the building it had replaced, it nestled the parsonage inside the L and the two buildings were separated only by a wide sidewalk. The membership was growing, visitors were being attracted, new programs were underway and my wife Kathleen and I were heart and soul in the action. In fact, among other things, Kathleen sang in the choir, taught a Sunday School class, and opened our home to overflow Bible study sessions. Whenever something was going on next door, one or the other of us was likely to be there.

But our family was humming with life too and increasingly the hums were in different keys. Our growing children, normally happy, began to seem too often out of sorts. Even minor stresses got them down and they cried easily and with little provocation.

They were getting lost in the shuffle and something had to change. After talking it over between us, my wife and I announced our plan: beginning that very week, we told the children, Friday night was going to be family night. I'd take no appointments. I'd stay away from the phone. Nothing short of an invasion from outer space would interfere. They met the news with a burst of glee.

Routines for this special night set up quickly. We popped corn and enjoyed brown cows — Pepsi over ice cream in tough kitchen tumblers. These were the basics of the evening. For the rest, we improvised. Sometimes we played table games. On chilly evenings, we might build a fire in the fireplace. Sometimes we broke out favorite books for reading, but we never went out on family night.

From the beginning the children looked forward to Friday, but not because we spent great sums of money on them or peppered them with thrills. Being together as a family seemed to be thrill enough. I believe our children had an easy-to-satisfy hunger for family life and because we attended to that need early, the results became a great resource for holding our family together.

Every father promotes "togetherness" in his own way. I never had a lathe in the basement or a boat in the backyard to be repaired. That sort of thing has not been my forte. I sometimes wish even yet I had had greater manual skill to share with the children. But every father has something of his own to give. I gave time and attention and those Friday nights made their own special contribution to our life together.

For us, even a Christian home was not all sweetness and light. It was a place where siblings rivaled each other and little wills collided, sometimes like freight trains. It was a place that could ring with laughter one moment and become clouded with tears the next. In our home little children lisped their first prayers at table and told their first lies. My wife and I sometimes went to bed distraught over a misdemeanor but arose to greet the new dawn with prayer and renewed hope.

Realism is the word for the Christian home. And realism is the word for the Christian father's approach to the task of fathering. Before my job as father was finished in its more active phases my endurance had been measured, my true values examined, my capacity to love stretched and stoical feelings unmasked, to show me I had a heart that could be as soft as whipped butter.

Fortunately, Kathleen and I were blessed from the start of our marriage with generous supplies of realism, bequeathed to us by our families, the church and a culture whose traditions were still fairly intact. We didn't marry with an exclusively romantic notion of marriage to guide us — the idea that wedded love must be unclouded bliss. We were romantic enough, mind you, enthralled with each other at twenty-one years of age, and we are still warmly in love at fifty-three. But realism has been the cornerstone.

We didn't discover realism; it was bequeathed to us. In 1947 the Christian marriage ritual used at our wedding called us to pledge ourselves to each other "for better, for worse; for richer, for poorer; in sickness and in health; to love and to cherish till death us do part." Marriage was for keeps and no eventuality was left out of the vows. Surprisingly, we learned across the years that this kind of unqualified commitment is the ground, the rock-hard base, for a lifetime of romance.

Carolyn came along to help us celebrate our first anniversary, Carolyn Dawn, that energetic five pound ten-ounce bundle who seemed to have a personality of her own from the first day. From the beginning, I substituted for her given names playful variants that popped out of my imagination as I sang to her — Carolinko, Linko, Klunko. (One that came later, Daught, she still uses in letters.) We were living just west of Toronto at the time in a one-room apartment. I was a part-time student and a marginal provider.

Then, when Carolyn was approaching three years of age, we moved, lock, stock and barrel, to Greenville, Illinois, where I was to finish two final years on a bachelor's degree. Lock, stock and barrel could all be packed into a steamer trunk bought at a Toronto secondhand store for $5. Affluence had not yet struck our society.

Three weeks after landing in Greenville, Donald arrived. That was October of 1951. And eight weeks before leaving Greenville, Robert was born. That was July of 1953. Don and Bob were like parentheses around my last two years of college.

I was twenty-seven by then and wondering if seminary training was within reach for a man of such advanced years with a wife and three children. A student pastorate became available in Lexington, Kentucky, a short drive from Asbury Theological Seminary, however, so we began to load what we owned into our bronze-colored Ford and in two trips moved it all to Lexington, 350 miles to the southeast. Three years of theological training were ahead — plus supporting a family, serving a church and giving some quality time to growing children.

Those three arduous years were possible only because my wife looked upon keeping a home and tending a family as a career. When you're a seminary student and approaching thirty, you don't exactly give off a macho male image to yourself or your wife. But what I was doing was important to both of us and Kathleen put forth her best, uncomplaining effort. My children and I are still the beneficiaries of that attitude.

Toward the close of my seminary days, John David came along. That was in April of 1956. Soon after his arrival we were invited to take a church in New Westminster, British Columbia, and we began to plan for our move to the parsonage. In August, we were to start across the continent like a family of pilgrims, in a turquoise-blue Plymouth towing a sturdy but springless trailer loaded five feet high from the bed. We jiggled and joggled for twenty-five hundred miles.

John David was a special child from the start. He was small, frail, and his cry was high-pitched. He cried a lot at night and that didn't go well with our efforts to move. In the middle of the night we took our turns rocking him in his carriage amid packing boxes in the living room of our Lexington apartment. At times he seemed unconsolable.

By the time we had been in Western Canada two months, the doctor there asked us if we would like to see a specialist. The specialist told us little after his preliminary examination but wanted to see John David again when he was one year old. Shortly after John David's first birthday, he asked us to take him to the Vancouver Children's Hospital for a full battery of tests. We left him there for three days, driving back to New Westminster in silence.

On the night of the third day, Dr. Dunn phoned. I was out at a board meeting; the children were in bed; the house was quiet; my wife answered the phone.

"You may come and get John David now," he said.

There followed a description of the findings. A few lesser matters and then came the jarring word that portions of John David's brain were not functioning and nothing could be done.

"Nothing?" my wife asked incredulously.

"Nothing," he said.

Dr. Dunn was a gentle and considerate man, but how do you tell a mother gently that her child is retarded and the retardation may turn out to be profound? Even though we had suspected what we were likely to learn, my wife was shattered by the news. In the silence of that parsonage, she expressed her anguish in her own way. I came home later to a wife who had grown silent. She gave me the news in measured tones but beneath the control was devastation.

It took us several weeks to come to terms with the news. Sometimes we talked; sometimes we were silent. Don't think we didn't ask, "Why?" And the question "Why us?" was aired too. It was a particularly distressing question to my wife until, she reminds me, one day I replied, "Why not us? We're not God's pets." That seemed to help her begin to accept what had happened, a process that went on in both of us for a long while.

When John David was nearly three, he was admitted to Woodlands School in New Westminster, a large institution for the retarded. The separation made the pain acute again, but for the first time in three years, we were able to sleep through the night without being up to try to soothe him and quiet his high-pitched cries. He has spent his years since in Woodlands.

So, one winter day we passed our fourth child into the arms of a white-clad nurse. Within three weeks of that day, Donald became mysteriously ill. He couldn't move without crying because of the pain in his joints. He was admitted to the Royal Columbian on an emergency basis and within two or three days we were told it was rheumatic fever. For ten weeks, day after day we drove past one institution where John David now lived to visit Donald in another.

Our assignment was complicated by the fact that during those ten weeks Donald withdrew from us until on several visits I could only make emotional contact by sitting on his bed and making up silly stories. They were about such things as earthworms who lived in a house remarkably like ours and had to go to the hospital for surgery so they would be short enough to get inside the house and close the door. Gradually, lying there in bed, his eyes would light up as his imagination took over. We figured out later that this seven-year-old had seen what had happened to John David and was probably angry at us for abandoning him too. But our response at the time was not to analyze.

Nevertheless, ours has been a happy home, often radiantly happy. Fun blew up in the strangest and simplest ways. When Carolyn was six and the boys younger, early in December she began to ask her mother teasingly what they would get for Christmas.

"A big fat potato," her mother replied off-handedly during one of the quizzings.

That Christmas morning there were three big fat potatoes among the gifts. But what makes the day memorable was the conspiracy that a six-year-old drew her mother into the same afternoon. Christmas was also my birthday and the two of them saw to it that among my gifts was a nicely wrapped shoe box holding a carefully packed big fat potato.

As a father, I believed in reasoning with my children, but within limits. For example, I would not reason with a four-year-old at a busy intersection if he didn't want to cross when the "walk" sign flashed on. I'd take that little hand and lead him firmly across. Reason might later be used to explain that in such situations, Dad has to be the captain and obedience is required.

Nor would I try very hard to reason with a child who was simply being cantankerous. None of us reasons well in a bad mood.

Moreover, when basic family requirements were at stake, I could not be reasoned out of them. For example, our children took piano lessons until the close of their second year in high school. After that it was up to each child whether or not to go on. This requirement was not negotiable and it led to the occasional unhappy moment. Nevertheless, we believe the rule was good because when the children knew that piano lessons were a part of what it meant to be a member of our family it helped them to summon their own wills to the task. They may have learned as much about discipline as about music.

When we got a television set in the early sixties, an old one given us by a parishioner, we limited the children's watching time to one-half hour a day during the week and one hour on Saturday. We had a rule about being home for meals on time too, but as the children got older we were flexible. Even so, early expectations made them considerate of their home and its schedule.

We had a curfew that was conservative during the week — ten o'clock — and slightly extended on weekends. This was in force during high school years and was subject to extension if circumstances warranted. Maybe the time set by a curfew is not so important as the fact that a curfew makes children feel answerable to parents. We also insisted, my wife especially, that we know where the children were at all times. After school, for example, they reported in.

We taught our children to respect one another's property. When we moved into a large parsonage where each had his own room, we made him sole custodian of the room. (I think reading Suzanna Wesley's rules for raising a family had lodged the idea in my mind.) No brother or sister was to enter without permission and possessions were not to be touched unless the owner agreed. This may seem severe but I believe they learned respect for the property of others by having their own and seeing it respected.

But in the application of these family expectations, I reasoned with our children about what we believed to be right for us all. One thing I learned was that reasoning styles must change as children grow toward adulthood.

When our children entered their teens (or perhaps slightly before) important changes began to take place in their way of seeing the world. They began to be aware of a growing independence from their parents. They went to activities farther away from home; later they drove cars. Moreover, their abilities in abstract thinking increased significantly and there was a growing skill in dealing with concepts, ideas, and perhaps most important, values.

It was a crisis time for everyone and I didn't escape the upheaval of it all. At times I felt panic. At times the easiest solution to the children's challenges seemed to be an unbending, authoritarian "No." In spite of these tendencies my major response to the crisis of adolescence was to dialogue with the children, reasoning with them within the structure of established family values.

My children remember that I took time to listen to them. For example, when Robert was fifteen I sensed a barrier developing between him and me. There had been no drop in his respect but only a growing sense of distance. One spring night I suggested we go for a walk and we walked all over Greenville. When I told him my concern, he was quick to explain what was bothering him.

"I just don't feel like a sinner," he told me. "I've tried to think of myself as vile and wretched, but I'm not."

I explained to him that a sinner is a person who wants to be independent from God; to go it alone. This frame of mind can exist in the most exemplary of people. The vileness may or may not come later but the impulse to hold one's life in independence from God is the core of all sin.

The talk was inconclusive because Robert needed time to think things through. But as we neared home, I felt the gap had been closed and I was satisfied for the time being. Two weeks later a noticeable change came in his spirit. He later told me that when a boy at high school had shot himself while playing with a gun in front of his friends, this had shaken him deeply. On his own, Robert committed his life to Jesus Christ.

Carolyn made her personal commitment to Jesus Christ first. She was twelve and I had preached one Sunday night from Galatians Five. She came forward in church, tears wet on her cheeks, and I had the privilege of being her spiritual as well as her physical father. With Don, the commitment took place in his bedroom where I had taken him for serious discussion about respect for his mother. He was sixteen.

These commitments to the Saviour were decisive; but before our children were born we had presented them to the Lord. In the fellowship of the church we had made public declaration of our intention to raise them for His glory. Three wonderful congregations shouldered that task with us and when the children sensed their own responsibility, they were simply affirming decisions that had been earlier made on their behalf.

Our children went through their teens in the nineteen sixties. For teenagers, that was the era of high anxiety and seething anger. Teens openly challenged adult values and there was little for the generations to agree upon. "Trust no one over thirty" was a widely quoted slogan; for them, middle class values were materialistic and what was right was something you decided from situation to situation. Television newscasts took viewers daily to the mayhem of the Viet Nam war in living color, and hundreds of thousands of young men in the United States lived under the shadow of the dreaded draft.

I remember this well because I was in Greenville where I had earlier finished my final two years of college. Now I was there as the college pastor. The college with nearly a thousand students had a conservative structure that kept youthful impulses for the most part within the bounds of acceptable conduct. There were no riots. But feelings were raw and it was hard to avoid verbal conflict. I remember standoffs between the generations even over the definition of such lofty Christian words as "mission" and "evangelism." A committee had met to plan a missions convention when this debate erupted. In the sixties, conflict was seldom out of sight.

It was not the easiest time in history to reason across generational lines. I was at a special advantage during those days, however, in that I was serving as a pastoral counselor to college young people. You can't listen sympathetically during the day and then go home and turn a deaf ear to your own teenagers. What young people wanted then (as now) I believe, was to be affirmed and respected by adults they admired.

In our family, positive relationships had been solidly established between parents and children in the first five years of each child's life. They were firmed up and reinforced in the remaining pre-teen years during camping trips, on evening visits to the Dairy Queen, while reading *Treasure Island* at the table after dinner, and even through the administration of a spanking for some misadventure.

If my fathering was effective during our childrens' adolescence, credit must be properly assigned. From the start, my wife put me in a good light with my children — no small factor in how they later responded to me. For example, when they were very small I would report to Kathleen by phone late in the afternoon that I had made my last pastoral call and would soon be home to eat. She would turn to the children and with excitement say, "Daddy's coming home!" Usually they met me gleefully at the door. I believe even so simple a procedure helped them develop positive feelings about me.

I belonged to a church that, from my perspective, was rightly conservative in its respect for biblical truth. The Bible's elevated view of fatherhood strengthened me in my efforts to be a Christian father, as well as helping the children to show honor.

Only because I had such supports was I able to reason with my children and field their adolescent challenges. And given the high status I had as a father, I could afford to give and take in the discussions which developed. I didn't have to fight for a place in their lives.

Once when family values were under inspection, Robert asked me why our family should need a second car. He was seventeen at the time and had been reading books about the energy crisis and ecology and the environment — books such as *Silent Spring*.*

Out on the driveway sat an eight-year-old khaki Ford Fairlane with 90,000 miles on its odometer. I had bought the car a couple of years earlier so that the children could get back and forth to campus, about one mile away. As the discussion developed, I agreed we could survive with one car but I suggested we lock the Fairlane for a two-week trial period before selling it. The children could use my car, I explained, whenever it was not in use. I made it clear that I had to have the car available at all times during working days and sometimes would need it at night for pastoral calls. Otherwise, they were free to use it. The experiment never even got underway.

But I didn't always come out so well in these family discussions. In 1971 I ordered a car for myself — a one-year-old Mercury with a big engine — to replace my 1969 model. This again raised the question of energy and ecology.

"Why do you need a big Mercury?" the children asked pointedly.

* Rachel Carlson, *Silent Spring*. (New York: Houghton-Miflin, 1962)

My reasons didn't stand up very well and before we were finished discussing it I felt compelled to cancel the order — the day after the dealer had notified me the car was available. I went instead to a mid-sized car and after that to a compact. I have since moved back to a used down-sized Chevrolet but I believe the whole sequence was affected by my willingness to be reasonable with children who had a fresh and more spartan view of life.

During those teen years we discussed everything — music (especially rock music), how one should use leisure time, how many material things one really needed, how Christians should use money, what does it mean to be in love, what is marriage all about — everything! I feel sure I passed along some good ideas to them but I also learned a lot in the exchange. I became convinced that you can't shut teenagers down with an authoritarian "no," and that they can't afford to accept the values of their parents without examining them. For us, our children's adolescence was a stressful time, but not chaotic.

By now it will be evident that we are a talking family. This began when the children were in bassinettes and continued by cultivation through the years. Even when adults were wringing their hands over the generation gap, I refused to let such a gap develop in our family. I insisted that siblings resolve differences that would not evaporate in the normal flow of life, and that they keep open to us too. It was a requirement, so we learned to talk.

One night when all three children were in college, they came home from Friday night social events within minutes of one another. Kathleen and I had gone to bed. First Carolyn came into our room and sat on Kathleen's side of the bed — to talk. Then Robert arrived and sat at the foot of the bed. Later Don came and sat on the floor, his back against a dresser. Comments about the evening tumbled over one another and my wife and I fought against the sleepiness we felt. Finally, too drowsy to stay awake any longer, my wife said, "You children have got to get to bed. Sometimes I wish there were more of a generation gap in our family."

Because of my own experiences, I feel sorry for young married men who decide not to have children. Recently I met a young, childless couple at a church family life weekend. That night I had spoken on the Christian father. At the close, the young man, about twenty-seven, said: "Well, you give me more confidence. My wife and I talk about starting our family, but don't go beyond that."

His wife broke in, "Yes, whenever I want to talk seriously you just make jokes."

"Because I'm afraid," he shot back at her.

It's probably true that some refrain out of fear and that some men shouldn't be fathers. But if that is determined by a prior assessment of capacity, none of us should. None of us starts out with the maturity or wisdom or skill or unselfish caring to be a good father. Becoming a father is the very experience that can bring us the wisdom and develop fathering skills as they are needed.

When I rocked a feverish year-old son, something good happened to me as well as to the child. Also when I got a glass of water for a little girl who couldn't yet say "drink." Or when I took a son to a service station rest room, or helped him remove a sliver from his foot, or wound up his wind-up truck, or played tag with him in the park.

I remember when a three-week-old daughter baptized me into fatherhood by spewing milk all over my shoulder and down the back of my coat. It was my fault. I hadn't yet got the rhythm of burping a baby and she was my teacher. I also remember, ten thousand experiences later, seeing that same daughter, diminutive and alert in cap and gown, graduate from college.

The memories are innumerable: teaching a girl to ride a bike and later to drive a car. (I took her out to the cemetery east of town and she kept confusing the turn indicator with the gear shift lever); teaching a boy how to shine his shoes; turning weeping into laughter with a bit of humor; sharing "knock-knock" jokes with eight-year-olds; making up limericks; watching pre-teen sons dive from a raft.

It's been expensive, I'll admit — piano lessons; French horn lessons; flute lessons; voice lessons; books; records; toys; doctor bills; the cost of sending a daughter to Europe as a college graduation gift; sending two boys a thousand miles to the Columbus Boy Choir Summer Camp in Princeton, New Jersey; orthodontic bills for all three children paid

for in installments that ran for who can remember how
many years. There were shoes and clothes to buy — and
more clothes and shoes. Where did the money come from?
I can't figure it out now. We lived on a minister's salary and
we lived frugally. But as careful as we've been about bor-
rowing, I'd go into debt for any of the above items. They
were all important; all a part of a master plan. All contributed to the joy of fathering.

Things can go wrong and they did. I remember the rise in
anxiety I felt when, a day after our five-year-old daughter's
tonsillectomy, the doctor told us she had to go back to the
operating room. Some bleeding had to be cauterized. It
seems like such a small thing now after twenty-one years
of visiting in hospitals where families were going through
bigger crises. But it was our child and the crisis was big to
us.

Lots of little things went wrong. In the course of raising a
family there were dented fenders and a visit to a high
school principal's office about a difficult son. (Even though
not all was perfect in the school, I told my son in the presence of the principal that I expected him to cooperate.)
There were long distance calls from young men in graduate
school requesting help to obtain another loan and calls
from a daughter in need of reassurance on her first full-
time teaching job.

The earliest signs of our childrens' impending adulthood
may have appeared when they lightheartedly parroted back
to me things I had often said to them in great seriousness:
"There's a right way to do everything" or, "remember life is
not a one-way street." They could say these things with
mock seriousness and just the right amount of patronizing
in their tones to shatter my composure and move me to
laughter. How pompous I must have sounded to teenagers.

We tried to take the practice of our faith seriously at
home. We taught our children to pray at bedtime, usually
by praying with them, and we taught them to thank God for
their food before each meal from the time they were old
enough to understand "patties up." When we traveled
together, as we did often in the summer, we usually began
the day by reading Psalm 91, the Traveler's Psalm.

We also read the Bible and prayed together as a family after the evening meal. I confess it got more difficult to keep the schedule as the children got older. School activities made their demands and the program at the church was full, with something for all ages. There were a few times when we got together with serious intent but something funny was said and we simply dissolved in laughter, leaving the devotions for the next day. Yet, we never gave up the ideal of family devotions.

Moreover, some devotional times were so rewarding that they made every failed effort seem worthwhile. I recall evenings when we read and prayed and then, because school pressures were lighter or holidays had come, the children, lounging on the living room floor, lingered to talk about their concerns, several times for more than an hour. As I mentioned earlier the ecology crisis and pollution perils were real anxieties to thinking teenagers. What better occasion to talk about their meaning?

Those devotional moments are high points in my memory. I sometimes laid the Bible aside and left the living room, feeling closer to God and my family than at any other time. My wife and children felt the same. Prayer introduced us to true family togetherness.

I can't say the religious emphases of our home were all on the positive side. After the children were grown, I once asked them what they remembered as most unpleasant about their childhood. "Sunday," Robert replied, and the others agreed. Then, they elaborated.

My wife taught Sunday School and sang in the choir. As the church outgrew its new facility we volunteered to open our home for overflow Sunday School classes — first we had one in a basement room, then a second one in the living room, and a third in the kitchen.

Sunday became more hectic for the children than we had realized. They reminded us in that later conversation that they had been awakened with urgency: "Get up and get dressed for Sunday School." I had already gone to my duties and the house needed some final touches to ready it for its regular Sunday morning use. From the time of arising until noon, the children reported, there was a sense of hurry that left Sunday a slightly tarnished day in their memories. I wish it had been otherwise but I don't feel guilty over the matter. Christian homes — including parsonages — can't be perfect. One of life's exercises is to learn to take the bad with the good (and in our home there was both bad and good to accept).

If we were going through that period again, I'm not sure much would be changed except that we would be a bit more attentive to the childrens' feelings. They were whole people — "persons" as we now say — and perhaps they needed more consideration on Sunday mornings. Perhaps we would try harder to see the day through their eyes.

We did a lot of forgiving in our family. We were probably not harder or easier on one another than members are in any other family, but our behavior expectations were high. A religious home almost unavoidably has high expectations and people of all ages being what they are often fall short. I wouldn't want to lower the expectations if we were doing it again. I think it's important to make children stretch; to be kind, polite, honest. But where there are high expectations, there has to be forgiveness.

I tried to set the pace by apologizing when I had erred. I went to my childrens' rooms on several occasions to say, "I can see I was unfair in my judgment," or "Forgive me for being harder on you than I needed to be." It was not that I felt apologetic for being a father or for exercising authority. That would have been a mark of weakness. I was apologizing for being unfair or insensitive. My daughter Carolyn tells me now that this was always more difficult for her to take than any punishment I had meted out; it usually brought tears to her eyes.

Our family policy was to take care of a matter when punishment was needed and then make clear to everyone concerned that the issue was closed. The children would never again be reminded of their wrongdoing after it had been righted.

Once when one of the boys was about twelve, my wife and I both became aware that he had been using his strong, verbal skills to shade the truth. We felt we were being deceived; if not lied to. But the shading was of a very high order. We watched this happening, compared notes, and then one day in the kitchen we cornered him and began asking for a reckoning.

At first he tried to talk his way out. But we were ready for that. You could see the look of dismay on his face as he realized that both his father and mother were solidly against him. We faced him with one instance after another. Gradually he backpeddled as we held him accountable to the truth as we perceived it. At the end he admitted we were right except for one situation. We believed him and conceded this one instance. In the whole exchange, there were no raised voices, just serious straight talk. And after he had apologized to both of us, I made it clear that when we stepped out of the kitchen the whole matter was closed.

We still get together as a family whenever we can. Just a short time ago, our son Don phoned to ask if he and his wife June could drop in to see us that evening. They live five miles south of us here in the west end of Metro Toronto. Our daughter Carolyn, and her husband Doug, who live two miles north of us, came along also — at Don's invitation we later learned.

The talk in the family room flowed easily with the sharing of news, a bit of humor, reports on how jobs were going and whatever else could be woven into the tapestry of conversation. During this pleasant time, subtly, with typical indirection, Don dropped the news that had occasioned the get-together: six months hence, he and June would make us grandparents. Carolyn and Doug had given us a similar announcement only three months earlier. The two infants will be three months apart.

We were overjoyed. That night, the message went by long distance telephone to Robert in St. Louis. We can scarcely wait. Except that I have just nicely got straight in my head what it means to be a father. Now I must start all over again and learn to be a grandfather.

*Remember, a gentleman is the next best character to a
Christian and the Christian includes the gentleman.*

William Carey, father of the
modern missionary move-
ment, to his son

Epilogue

I promised early in this book that there would be no lectures, no preaching or pomposity. I don't intend to break that promise now. However, some principles of Christian fathering have become clear to me and I'd like to nail them down for the help they may be to other fathers besides myself.

Clarification has come from three major sources. First of all, from the down-to-earth narratives of my four friends. In addition, during this past year the Bible's implicit and explicit views on the subject have become more plain. And, finally, some of my past experiences with families in which father-child relationships had broken down have organized themselves more clearly in my thinking.

I now share these principles — as briefly as I can write them.

•*"Father" is an honorable title and Christian fathers should bear it with distinction.*

Jesus addressed God repeatedly as "Father." This alone should make father an honorable word to all Christians.

The elevation of the title permeates the Judeo-Christian faith. Consider, for example, its place in the Ten Commandments. The first four laws (You shall have no other gods beside Me; do not profane My name, etc.) are religious in emphasis, the last five (Do not kill; do not steal, etc.) are social. Between the two categories, almost as a bridge, is the command to "Honor your father and your mother. . . ."

This command is an integral part of the moral law of God. Team parenting is certainly implied, but father is named first, reflecting the biblical sense of his headship in family matters.

I mention this not to imply that father is more important than mother in the family. To argue who is *more* important is a fruitless quibble. Nor is this a plea that father be put on a pedestal. The commandment reflects that to be a father is to hold an honorable and responsible position in the life of the family.

It seems to me that cultural drift has taken us in an opposite direction. We are much more inclined to speak of "mother and father" than of "father and mother." Subtle though the switch is, it tends to move father toward the periphery of family life, with certain predictable consequences. One writer on marriage and the family, Dr. N.W. Ackerman, calls father "the forgotten man" today. Others equally informed have referred to him as the phantom parent. For family health and solidarity, father needs to stand with mother at the center of things. To do so, he must bear his title with dignity.

•*Fathers need reinforcement if they are to fulfill their biblical mandate, giving leadership to the family.*

One thing that stood out as I began to read the manuscripts which became the chapters of this book was that each of the fathers had been blessed by God's gift of a supportive wife. I know all five women personally. They are gentle and empathetic and at the same time wise and strong. They are also the kind of women who seem to complement their husbands rather than compete with them. Parenting, I know, requires mutual support. Mother's role is in some respects more demanding than father's and she fares poorly if his support is not strong and dependable.

But this summary is in reference to fathers and therefore the support they need must be highlighted. The fathers in this book were affirmed by their wives. I assume that when their children were growing up, differences of opinion relative to parenting were worked out behind the scenes. They certainly were in our home. But in the face-to-face family experiences, fathers received visible support for their leadership roles.

Add to a wife's support the reinforcement of a loving and ordered Christian congregation and a father's likelihood of doing well is greatly increased. However, a yearly Father's

Day observance is not enough. The biblical mandate must be worked out in sermon and seminar, in consultation and counseling until affirmative attitudes pervade the congregation and fatherhood receives the recognition God intended.

●*Christian fathering succeeds only when it is grounded in the spiritual realities of our faith.*

We tend to assume today that there's a method for every task and if the right method is used the task will succeed. Humanism says, "Man can do it." Pragmatism says, "It's the method that matters." Therefore well-meaning fathers within the church may pick up such viewpoints and determine to master the right methods and in so doing raise the perfect family.

The problem is that such humanistic thinking is partial. It ignores clear biblical realities. The Scriptures say, "For we are not contending against flesh and blood, but against the principalities, against the powers, against the world rulers of this present darkness, against the spiritual hosts of wickedness in the heavenly places." (Ephesians 6:12 RSV.) In words like these, the Scriptures often describe the spiritual forces that set themselves against everything good — including the Christian family.

I read John Benson's recollections and I see him as a father concerned both with practices and prayers. The Christian father must be a praying man who, in moments of privacy, goes to his knees again and again for wisdom and strength. He should also lead his family in daily prayers and faithful church attendance since these too are ways of acknowledging the spiritual realities in which family life is grounded. John apparently tried to wed good sense and spiritual resources.

●*It's a Christian father's high privilege — and duty — to love his wife.*

In the great New Testament passage on the Christian family, Ephesians 5:21 to 6:4, the apostle gives more than three times as much attention to husband-wife relationships than to those between parents and children. Apparently the relationship of parents to each other is the greatest single factor in determining the success of a Christian home. It's noteworthy, further, that in Paul's four-fold instructions, the greatest number of words are directed to the husband regarding his love for his wife. This should register upon us with force when we remember the low view of womanhood in the culture of the first century.

Paul's instructions are psychologically sound. Respect between parents reduces tension and increases security in the home. Moreover a father's deferential treatment of his wife in front of the children elevates their mother before them and sets a model for the next generation to follow. Someone has said, "The greatest gift a man can give his children is to love their mother."

•*A Christian father takes seriously the fact that the first five years of a child's life are crucial.*

The foundation for ongoing father-child relationships is laid during the earliest years. It's also during these years that a child's sexual identity is formed. In fact, students of the origin of homosexuality seem more and more inclined to hold this view. In addition, a child's sense of self-worth is established in the first five years, as are his basic skills in relating to other humans.

The late Margaret Mead, an anthropologist, character-ized fatherhood as a social invention. A man, that is, may give paternity to a child without even knowing the child. A woman cannot give maternity on the same terms. Her life is profoundly and irreversibly affected, even if she seeks abortion or puts the child up for adoption. Fatherhood, therefore, is relatively more social than biological and this leaves the father with more freedom to choose how deeply involved he will be with his child.

The Christian father, however, cannot comfortably choose a limited involvement. Paternity, to him, is an act of procreation. That is, it is an actual participation with God in the creation of a unique human life. No Christian father who knows this can take lightly the arrival of his child. Moreover, since to him fathering involves the guidance of an eternal soul toward God, his assignment is an act of stewardship, in partnership with his wife.

It seems to me that during the first five years of a child's life, a Christian father should enter readily into family nurturing, rocking the infant, sharing in the feeding task, getting on the floor with a one-year-old, taking a three-year-old for exploratory walks, and through a thousand such experiences laying the groundwork for the child's trust and obedience in the years ahead.

•*A Christian father must fill the role of a leader.*

I have been baffled often by resistance to the idea that the home needs a leader and it should be the father. This resistance may arise from misunderstanding or caricature of the father's role. What makes it baffling, however, is that leadership is a key subject in every other realm of life — education, business, politics, the church. We are constantly admitting that the strength of an organization hinges on its leadership.

I hold, in spite of the resistance, that the home needs the leadership of a father and that a wise Christian father will think this matter through as early in the fathering task as possible. He will need to make several points of clarification. For example, a man can be a parent without being a tyrant. He can be both a pal and a parent, two distinct elements in a rich father-child relationship. A noisy father is not necessarily a strong father. Noise, in fact may signal his rejection of the role or panic over his feelings of incompetence. "Macho" is not what his family needs most.

There's more than one style of leadership for the home. In a democracy like ours, participatory leadership may work well. That is, a father doesn't have to function as an autocrat and boss. He can take the family into decisions, so long as this is not a subtle way of abdicating his leadership. Abdication, however subtle, always creates a vacuum which mother or children tend, out of anxiety, to move to fill. The usual sign of abdication is some degree of domestic chaos.

It's helpful to remember that leaders in all walks of life make mistakes. That fact has been reinforced in this book. All five of us talk about ours. Mistakes are inevitable for humans. Wise leaders, however, face their mistakes with humility, make whatever amends they can, and carry on.

A father's leadership does not need to be jeopardized when he faces his mistakes. In apologizing to a child or spouse, for example, he need not abdicate his leadership role. Children recognize authenticity when they experience it. By the time they are in their mid-teens in fact, they are much more inclined to accept the leadership of a sincere and caring father who sometimes errs than of a father who is out of touch with his own weaknesses and eccentricities. In leadership, sincerity and strength go together.

•*A Christian father shows love for his children by respecting them.*

Respect is fundamental to love. So the Christian father begins early to respect his children. Even his respect for an infant's first "dolly" carries a message deeper than the act itself.

A father who respects his child's feelings is contributing to the child's mental health. Very early, children feel hostile, angry and frustrated just as readily as they feel happy. Even during an exercise in the discipline of a four-year-old, a father may acknowledge this fact by saying, "I know this makes you angry but you must do as I say." That recognition of a child's dark feelings is a gesture of respect for the child as a person.

A Christian father respects his childrens' opinions by listening to them. Fathers who listen carefully to their children in the early years of their lives are usually listened to by their children when the teen years arrive. During those later years conversations may get lively at times and opinions may collide with brain-jarring force. But if a groundwork of fatherly respect has been laid, conversations do not usually cease to take place.

Christian fathers respect their children's bodies. Whatever methods of enforcing discipline are used, it is *never* necessary to bruise a child. Punishment that is consistent and applied as soon after the offense as possible seldom needs to be severe. Bruising is a form of overkill. And withering scorn heaped on a child is an emotional equivalent to bruising. Both scar the psyche.

A Christian father should respect the body of a daughter as well as a son. The approach of young womanhood brings with it a mysterious sense of privacy. If a father has been wholesomely affectionate during the early years, this need not end. Families differ in the degree and manner of showing physical affection. But the father who steps over an invisible line, invading his daughter's sense of privacy by suggestion or force, commits the ultimate indignity against her. She will never fully recover.

There is growing evidence that incest is a more common (or more publicly known) experience in the lives of young people than has been thought heretofore. As a pastor, I've listened to confessions that were wrenching to give. I know the devastation, sometimes life-long, this kind of disrespect brings. Whatever damages a person so profoundly is opposite to love.

•*A Christian father realizes that his child bears a mysterious dignity neither he nor his wife can take credit for.*

In the ultimate sense, every child is a gift from God. Young parents perceive this to some degree when an infant comes into their lives, whatever the strength of their faith in God. I have witnessed it often in the maternity ward. Even unbelieving parents usually feel very close to God in the hours following the marvel of birth.

The little one comes not only as a gift from God but bearing God's mysterious likeness as well. Theologians refer to this as "the image of God in man." This makes the child much more than merely an extension of his parents or a means through which parents can fulfill their unrealized dreams. To a father, a child is neither an idol nor a plaything but rather a sacred trust. He owes his biological origin to his parents but his "being" to the God of all creation whose image he bears.

The wondrous dignity a child bears manifests itself in such matters as the mystery of the human will. There are clear hints of this when a two-year-old learns the force of "no." Later, as he surges toward adulthood he works out the issues of his own identity, choosing the kind of person to be and the kind of work to do. In unspeakably sad situations the child may set himself against all the values of a father, rebelling against both God and his parent.

Because of this mystery of the human will it is impossible to assure Christian fathers that their children will honor them and follow in their footsteps. Many a sincere Christian has been crushed to learn his child is incorrigibly set against what he himself holds precious. But we dare assume that the more fully a father works with God in carrying out his task — reinforced by family and church and to some extent society — the more likely the child is to grow up to honor him. Christian fathering is an act of faith daily renewed.

• *A Christian father should take delight in his children.*

A Roman Catholic entertainer being interviewed on a talk show was asked if he were proud of his children. He said, "No, I'm not, because pride is sin. I rejoice in my children." The difference is subtle, but real. In rejoicing in his children, a Christian father enjoys all that is admirable in his offspring and at the same time gives glory to God.

It is too much to expect that he will rejoice in everything they do, but neither does he rejoice in everything he himself does. He may have moments of deep disappointment, especially when in his children he catches glimpses of his own likeness. One of my teachers once said, "In our children, we meet ourselves coming back." But these darker lines aside, a Christian father can learn to identify good traits and laudable skills in his children and take delight in them. Every child senses whether he is fundamentally a trial or a treasure to his father.

• *Finally, a Christian father should draw on the joy of the Lord for his strength.*

Jesus Christ is the Lord of a Christian home and wherever he is honored, there is joy. Of course, a home can be unified without giving loyalty to him. In fact, you will sometimes see more harmony in a non-Christian home than in one that is Christian. The reason is that the home is a human institution before it is a Christian institution and when human domestic laws are followed, harmony results. But the joy of the Lord is a plus factor and only those homes that live in submission to the Lord live in the experience of his joy.

We fathers need to think hard about this. If we are strong persons, we may feel that submitting ourselves to Christ is somehow unmasculine. If we suspect we are weak we may feel that to do so is to increase our weakness. Both ideas are false. Masculine strength is enhanced by loyalty to the only one who was a fully and untarnished human — Jesus the Christ. And he can be counted on to bring out the best in those fathers who lack confidence in themselves. In either case, the result is joy.

When I read the story of Paul Ellis conversing with his sons on the golf course, I felt joy. When I pictured W. Dale Cryderman submitting to the frivolity of his boys on a northern camping trip, the sensation this brought was joy. When I recall Hugh White carrying out discipline with a switch that broke, sending both parties into laughter, I felt joy. I experienced a surge of joy when I imagined the Benson family singing hymns together. These were all special moments, to be sure. But nothing in Christian family life needs to escape the joy of the Lord. Even when we are sorrowing, the apostle Paul said, we are always rejoicing.

We Christian fathers don't do everything right, for sure, but we do one thing right every time we remember that the joy of the Lord is our strength.